FREE TO SERVE

DENNIS A. MCINTYRE

FREE TO SERVE

Bennett books may be ordered through booksellers or by contacting:

Bennett Media and Marketing
1603 Capitol Ave., Suite 310 A233
Cheyenne, WY 82001
www.thebennettmediaandmarketing.com
Phone: 1-307-202-9292

ISBN: 978-1-957114-14-9 (sc)
ISBN: 978-1-957114-15-6 (e)

Printed in the United States of America

Bennett Media rev. date: 04/08/2022

ABOUT THE AUTHOR

Dennis A. McIntyre is a native of Rochester, NY, and served as an electrical engineer and a technical writer for over 40 years before retiring. Since retirement, Dennis has focused his efforts on his personal writing, publishing his first book; an autobiographical work entitled *Legacy of Love*, in 2008 through Tate Publishing. Dennis currently resides in Dacula, GA, and attends Anchor Church in Grayson, GA. He enjoys using his gifts of encouraging and writing for the glory of God's kingdom. His main goal for writing involves drawing people into closer relationships with the Lord and one another.

This work is a continuation of Jake Wilson's story from "Freedom's Journey."

Contents

REFLECTION

The journey for Jake and his family seemed more like something out of a fairy tale than reality. The old farmhouse had become the Wilson family's new home. The major remodeling was complete. Nicole and Alicia shared a bedroom, while Matt and Diana had their own rooms. Brandon moved into the room where he had stored his handmade chest of drawers. Terry and Jake enjoyed the privacy of their room with a large walk-in closet and master bath. The apartment, which seemed so crowded, was now replaced with a home several times larger.

Jake sat on a two-person swing hung from the front porch ceiling. Brandon built it and surprised Terry and Jake shortly after they moved into the house. To Brandon it was a house-warming present, but Jake treasured the gift beyond words. He would sit on it on warm evenings and reflect on all that God had done in his life. The renewed relationship with his long lost son, Brandon, was proof that God had been in control all along. The swing was built with love and the quality of its construction went well beyond anything found on the market. Brandon had learned the carpentry trade well from his uncle. Now, the young man was working full time with Jake in the plumbing business. As Jake slowly moved back and forth on the swing, his thoughts were filled with praise for the miracles in his life.

The sun was setting and the wisps of clouds on the horizon were bright with brilliant browns and reds. The reflection caused Jake's face to warmly radiate the joy that he also felt in his heart. He called to Terry to come out and enjoy the moment with him.

"What a sight, Terry. Isn't God wonderful?"

"I can't believe we are in this house."

"Someone needs to pinch me. I must be dreaming."

"The children love their rooms. Now they can invite their friends over as well."

"Yeah, that was a problem with the apartment. There was little room for us let alone guests."

"Brandon has been a terrific asset to the business as well. He is like a sponge, absorbing everything that I try to teach him about the plumbing business. Sometimes, he even shows me some things. God has truly blessed my work."

"We are so blessed."

Terry snuggled close to her husband on the swing. The sun disappeared, leaving a host of stars brightly glowing in the relatively clear sky. Jake stared into the night sky as if to see something specially meant for him. The blessings that he now enjoyed left him with expectations of what was in the future. He wondered if all that he had been given would soon be taken away. Certainly, the life that he led growing up through his teen years did not warrant rewards. The months that he served in prison were due punishment for his actions.

"Terry, do you think this is all a dream? I feel so undeserving of everything."

"Did Jesus deserve to go to the cross?"

"Of course not. He did it for us. We deserved punishment for our iniquities."

"Jesus went through the anguish of the cross to prove to His creation that He loves us. Much like the fact that you don't feel you

deserve the things you have been given, Jesus did not deserve the pain He suffered."

"Yeah, but there must be a catch."

"Jake Wilson! You can't stop talking about the things God has done in your life. You are a witness in the words you speak and the life you are living. I think God is honoring you for that."

"I love Him. My life was truly a mess without Jesus. My testimony is also my praise for all He has brought me through, including being introduced to you."

"My life has turned around since I accepted Christ as well. My love for you has reached depths that I never imagined before. Somehow, I felt that I deserved the abuse from my first husband, but God has opened my eyes to see myself as His child. I feel so blessed.

"So then, what plans do you think God has for us?"

"We are all here for a reason. Life's journey may be to find our purpose."

Terry's words pierced Jake's thoughts, and he jumped up from the swing.

"I'll be right back, honey."

Jake went into the house and returned a moment later with his Bible. He opened it to one of the tabs where Judge Carter had underlined scripture. The verse was Ephesians 2:10. Jake began to read the words aloud.

"For we are God's workmanship, created in Christ Jesus to do good works, which God prepared in advance for us to do."

"Judge Carter read these words to me before sentencing me to prison. I read them over and over many times before. What do you think the good works are?"

"You are a wonderful father. Our children are very blessed to have you as their father. Perhaps, just being a great dad and nurturing our children is your work. Each one has accepted the Lord and received baptism."

Terry's words brought a stream of tears to Her husband's eyes. The knowledge that his children were following Jesus stirred such an emotional response. The idea that Jake could be a good father seemed in stark contrast to the father who abandoned him shortly after his fifth birthday. For many years, gangs, drugs and alcohol were Jake's family. As he thought about his role of fatherhood, Jake had to give all credit to the God who saved him. Somehow, God performed an amazing work in Jake's life. The love of a heavenly father was evident in Jake's life as an earthly one. Still, he wondered about other works that God had for him to do.

"I have come a long way as a father."

"You are also a great husband and provider."

"Despite the recession we are in, honey, I am blessed with abundant work. Every time I begin to wonder about what jobs are on the horizon, doors open."

"I think that God honors your commitment. We have always tithed, even when the money was not in the checking account. You wrote the check with such expectancy and He never let us down."

"That has been a source of strength. We cannot out give God. Each time the check was written, the monies appeared, often from clients that were delinquent. Some of them were on my 'give up on ever receiving payment' list."

"Perhaps, God was pricking their hearts as well."

"He must have, because I stopped trying. Still, it's hard to get a grasp on being chosen in advance to do good works for the Creator of the universe."

"When the time comes, you will know what additional things God has for you to do, Jake. One thing that I know for sure is that your work is not over."

"I want to serve Him daily. Whatever He has for me to do, I hope I can please Him."

"He will not give you anything to do that you are not equipped for. Don't worry about that, Jake Wilson."

Jake reflected back on all that had happened in his life. Surely, God's hands were on him. The tests that he seemed to endure were now part of his testimony. Perhaps, God would use those experiences to help others going through similar things. One think was certain. It was no accident that Jake had come to this place in his life. Brandon's reunion was proof of that.

Jake embraced Terry on that swing and shared their thoughts openly to each other. Terry loved to listen to whatever was on her husband's mind. Jake felt her joy with each gentle tap on his thigh or caress on his cheek. The destructive life that Jake had lived before their union was gone forever. God had worked a miracle in both of their lives, and they acknowledged that fact.

THE CAMPFIRE

A lthough most of the farm had been sold to a housing contractor, Jake's land was still several acres in size. Old Betsy continued to be used to pull the trailer full of hay during the autumn months for the children and their friends. During one of those events, a friend from Alicia's Wednesday night class at church enjoyed the hayride. She said that her parents used to own a farm in upstate New York and would take a wagon full of kids to the pumpkin patch to select one to take home. At the end of the evening, her father would light a fire in an open field well away from anything flammable. Cooking marshmallows and making smores with chocolate covered graham crackers was a welcomed treat. The idea sounded like fun for Brandon, but Jake's experience with fire was disastrous. Two fires (Hawaii and Virginia) had been etched in his mind as a child, consummated by the wrath of his stepfather.

Brandon tried to convince Jake that having a small bonfire on the property could be a great outreach, especially for families. Somehow, the idea had far less appeal to Jake who vividly recalls the catastrophic damage caused by the lighting of a few leaves as a young boy. There was a large cleared area on the property, well away from the house and barn that could be used. The only question was whether the town would allow it and what restrictions would be required if the town gave the okay. Brandon was convinced that a well-supervised bonfire with fellowship was part of his calling to serve in his earthly ministry. Convincing Jake of that might take some doing, but Brandon felt a strong urge to pursue the idea.

Bob would often visit to fire up Old Betsy and enjoy one of Terry's delicious home cooked meals. He was always welcomed and treated as family. Brandon invited him to come over for dinner one night, after discussing the idea with Terry. Bob knew many people on the town board and could help get Brandon's questions about having a bonfire on the premises. Terry encouraged Brandon to pursue the matter as well. After dinner that night, Brandon took his uncle to the spot where he had envisioned a fire.

"I would like to create a pit or something over here, Uncle Bob. What do you think?"

"I don't think the town will object to the location, as it is well away from the things that might catch fire. How big an area do you have in mind?"

"I want it big enough for several families to roast marshmallows with their kids at the same time. We could dig a pit about ten feet square and fill it with concrete."

"Why concrete?"

"Well, I was thinking that it would be easier to clean up later while providing a stable surface for the fire."

"I can contact a friend on the board to get his input."

"That would be great. I was also thinking about setting the pit about a foot or so below ground level. The dirt removed could be piled up around the perimeter as a way to ensure the fire is well contained."

"That's a great idea. How much digging do you think we need to do?"

"We?"

"If I can get the okay, I can get the dozer and help."

"That would be wonderful. If the town agrees, then we need to find out how big the pit needs to be to support a ten-foot square fire.

I can envision people sitting at least one row around the perimeter just outside the pit level. We can include a drainage ditch towards the creek to keep the pit free of rain water."

"You seem to have spent a lot of time thinking about this?"

"I would like to use it as a ministry. Aunt Bertha would like that, don't you think?

"That she would. That she would."

Bob made a rough sketch of the site to present to the town board along with a list of questions to ask. The two men returned to the house. Jake and Terry were sitting on the front porch swing waiting for them to return.

"So what have you boys been up to?"

"BJ and I were just passing a few thoughts around. He sure is enjoying it here." Bob said this to skirt the issue of the fire.

"We love it here as well. We owe it all to you."

"I was just honoring an old woman's last wishes. Bertha must be smiling down from her heavenly home, especially seeing you united with BJ."

"By the way, did you see what I added to the barn?"

"What's that, Jake?"

"First, I had a new electric panel installed. I think we have more power available there than in the house."

"I guess you plan on using some tools and making the barn into a workshop."

"Just a small section, Bob. Don't worry. You will still be able to do your thing there as well. I also had some lighting added. You can come out and putter at night now."

"Sounds great."

Brandon motioned to Bob to go to the barn with Jake and to view the changes. Bob understood that Brandon desired to spend some time alone with Terry. Jake was just as eager to show the electrical changes anyway, so getting him away from Brandon was not a problem. Bob knew that he needed to keep

Jake occupied at the barn to allow Brandon the time that he needed with Terry. When they were well out of earshot, Brandon took a seat beside Terry on the swing.

"I'm glad to have a moment to talk with you alone, Terry."

"What is it, Brandon? By the way, your dad and I sure enjoy this swing."

"I'm so glad to know you guys enjoy it. It faces the sunset as well."

"Last night it was breathtaking."

"I have been driven to start a ministry. I am not sure about everything yet, but I feel led to build a fire pit towards the back of the property near the creek."

"A fire pit?"

"The thought started during one of the hayrides. Do you remember Alicia's friend, Joanie?"

"I remember."

"She talked about the warm memories with her father around a camp fire toasting marshmallows. I think we can create memories like that for families here in Florida."

"Jake has different memories when it comes to fire."

"I know. That is why I am glad he is not here right now. We may need to break it to him later. Anyway, Uncle Bob will help me get the details if the town will let us build a pit."

"When would you want to have a fire?"

"I'm thinking once a month during the autumn and, perhaps, a little more frequently during the cooler winter months."

"Have you thought about where you would get the wood to burn?"

"I have contacted some places that throw out old pallets. These are all made of hard woods and great for long lasting burning. Many of these places said they would stack the pallets for me, instead of placing them in their dumpsters. We could also have some fire wood delivered."

"You seem to have things worked out pretty well so far. Let me know what the town says. Then I will discuss it with Jake."

"I will and thanks for listening."

"My pleasure. I enjoy sharing with all my children."

Brandon smiled. His dream had begun to take hold, at least until the town had its say on the matter. He knew that if anyone could convince Jake that the idea was good, it was Terry. Just a gentle pat on the back from her, and Jake would immediately calm down.

Bob looked back at the house and could see Brandon sitting alone on the swing. Terry had gone into the house to check on the children, so it was time to head back from the barn. Bob was also pleasantly surprised by the lighted workshop that Jake had made just for him. It was complete with an assortment of tools used to maintain the tractor. Bob could come out to the farm whenever he desired.

"That was a great tour. That workroom is just the thing I need. I don't know why I didn't do that earlier."

"You talked about it. I just wanted to do something special for you."

"That was very special, indeed. Very special."

"I'm glad you like it. Some men don't want others to move their tools, if you know what I mean."

"That is not a problem for me. I can never remember where I put them."

"Now they have a place and so do you."

"Thanks, Jake. I love it. Now let's go see if Terry has any pie left."

"You got her pegged pretty well, Bob. She tries to keep something on hand for guests, that is if the kids don't get to it first."

"You mean, 'Big kids' don't you?"

Jake could not hold back his sheepish grin. The spare tire around his waistline added further evidence. As the two men reached the house, Terry came out with a freshly baked pan of brownies.

"I swear that woman can read my mind."

"We were just talking about having some baked treat, honey."

"Bob is a special guest. Brownies are easy, and I put them in when I heard he was here. You better help yourself, Bob, before the kids smell the aroma."

"You bet I will. Thanks."

"You are so welcome. You are always welcome here."

Terry's words only served to reinforce Jake's. Bob felt like part of the family, and it felt good. He knew that he had made the right decisions on behalf of Bertha in the handling of her property. Her legacy to help people would live on in the lives and hearts of the Wilson family. Feeling like being part of that family warmed Bob's heart as well. Having the freedom to come out at anytime held enormous joy as well.

"If you guys need anything further, give Jake or me a shout. We need to spend some quality time with the kids."

"I'm good, Terry," Bob responded.

"Me too," Brandon added.

Bob grabbed one last brownie for the road and started heading towards his truck. Brandon followed.

"So BJ. How did Terry respond to the bonfire plan?"

"Great, Bob. I think she could hear the excitement in my voice. She wants me to pursue it further, so I guess we just need to hear what the town board has to say now."

"I will check that out this week. I'll be in touch."

"Thanks so much, Uncle Bob. I really appreciate it."

"I'll be calling you later when I know something. Keep the faith."

"You bet."

THE YOUTH GROUP

T he following Wednesday morning came quickly. Brandon would have overslept if Jake had not rapped on his door.

"Time to get up Brandon. You must have forgotten to set your alarm, it's nearly seven."

"Huh," Brandon said somewhat groggy.

"I said, take a quick shower, grab a bite and go. We have work to do."

"I'll be right there, Dad."

It was unusual for Jake to be up before Brandon who was an early riser. Brandon had been up most of the night thinking about the possibilities of a small group ministry around a fire. The thoughts included music, story telling, and a lot of good old-fashioned laughter. Each time that he tried to fall asleep, something else seemed to add to the mix of potential options. He didn't play an instrument and thought about friends who did. He was blessed with a good singing voice, but never led a group. If music was to be included, then he had work to do to find volunteers to help. The possibilities continued to flow well into the night. Yet, despite the lack of restful sleep, Brandon was fully alert that morning. It was as if God had given him a recharge of energy. Although, Jake felt that he might crash at work before the day ended, Brandon was not slothful.

The church had a series of midweek activities, including several adult Bible studies, a teen worship service, and something for the younger kids. Matt enjoyed a small group with other kids his age, while Diana, Nicole, and Alicia enjoyed the high-energy worship time. The teen group had a rag-tag band of kids playing drums, guitar, keyboard, and an occasional harmonica. The music they enjoyed could be heard on Christian contemporary radio, but most adults might not find it quite as recognizable. Somehow, God heard it and was pleased. They were offering sincere praise in their own way.

Brandon often spent some time with the teens before going to one of the adult groups on Wednesdays. He wanted to let his siblings know that he supported them, but an hour was more than his ears could handle. That Wednesday was unique, however. Brandon stood in the back of the large room where the teens met and still entertained thoughts of the bonfire. The loud sounds of the band did not seem as noisy. Before long, he found himself staying with them for the entire time.

About twenty minutes into the service, the music stopped. Brandon had always left before that, so he did not know what went on afterwards. One of the teens, a young man named Jason, went up on the stage and began to share his testimony. A pin could be heard hitting the floor due to the silence. Each attendee listened reverently as Jason spoke. Brandon was moved to tears as the words flowed. Jason had a story to tell about how he came to know the Lord, and God's Spirit was moving among them. What a testimony. The wheels of subconscious thought rolled inside Brandon's mind. It was just the ingredient that was needed at a bonfire. The warmth of the flames would be nothing compared to the words shared.

When Jason finished, there was an eerie silence. Tears were flowing, and each teen embraced Jason as he made his way towards them. The moment was special for them and even more for Brandon who had grown up most of his life without a father. To see such an outpouring of love, affection, and acceptance deeply moved him. He watched in awe.

Then something else happened which made the moment even more special. The band members took their places on the platform. Brandon anticipated a burst of high-octane music, but only the guitar and keyboard began to softly play. "Amazing grace, how sweet the sound that saved a wretch like me…" These kids were all singing in unison one of the most powerful hymns ever written. Brandon sang along with them, but was surprised when they sang several verses without any help from an overhead projection. They were reverently worshipping with Jason and praising God for his majesty. What a moment!

Brandon was moved beyond words. These kids were alive and God was their source of strength. They had a message for the world, unlike anything the adult ministries had heard or seen before. Surely, this was God speaking to Brandon who waited near the back door to greet each person as they left. His eyes were still red with tears when Jason approached.

"*Thank you, young man, for sharing your testimony. God loves you.*"

"*He loves all of us.*"

"*My name is Brandon.*"

"*I am Jason.*" They embraced.

"*Is this the first time that you shared your story, Jason?*"

"*At this church it is, but I share whenever I have the opportunity.*"

"*Did someone ask you to share tonight?*"

"*No. This was my first time here. My neighbor invited me. I think he wanted me to share. Anyway, he told the worship leader that I would. Then he let me know when to go up.*"

"*Would you share with a group of people at my house if I asked you?*"

"*I am not ashamed to share. Sure I would.*"

That was a moment of confirmation for Brandon of what God had in store for him to do. If the bonfire idea worked out, then sharing how people came to know Christ was definitely a part of the scenario. The guitar player reached out his hand to Brandon as he approached.

"Hi. My name is David Richards, what's yours?"

"Brandon."

"Great to have you here tonight, Brandon."

"I am so glad that I stayed for the full service. Usually, I leave during the music. Diana, Nicole, and Alicia Wilson are my brothers and sisters."

"Great kids. They love the Lord."

Those words seemed strange to Brandon's ears. Often, the talents people possess or other abilities define them, but David recognized them by their eternal relationship. Brandon wondered how he perceived people. Then he wondered if anyone would say those words about him. He truly loved the Lord, but the question of whether it was evident on his face, could only be answered by someone else. Still, the words were uplifting and powerful.

"I want to ask you something, David."

"Ask away."

"I am toying with the idea of a family or group ministry at our home and wanted to know if you could help with your talents."

"What talents are you referring to, Brandon?"

"Guitar playing, namely, and leading some singing"

"So what's this plan of yours?"

"I live on a small farm. I am looking into the possibility of doing some hayrides during the autumn months."

"That sounds like fun."

"Yeah, well at the end of the ride would be a bonfire, at least if we can get the town's approval."

"My dad used to have campfires when we were growing up. They were fun. We sang, told stories, and laughed a lot. Mainly we laughed a lot."

"That's exactly the atmosphere that I want to create. Did you make smores as well?"

"We made them last week over the grill. I really like your idea."

"So, David, will you help lead in song if I can get it off the ground?"

"You bet. I may have a few friends who can help as well."

"That would be wonderful. I will keep in contact with you as I know more."

"Now, I am excited."

"One more thing. How often do you have people give their testimony on Wednesday nights?"

"Usually, someone comes forward every week. Sometimes, we have more than one. These kids bond with each other by sharing. I think that if no one volunteered I could call on any number of people to share again. Besides, there are always new people attending who never heard before."

"You mean like me?"

"Yeah! Thank you for asking. I look forward to hearing from you."

SUPPER AT THE WILSON'S

T hat evening was a milestone in Brandon's life. It reinforced God's plan to use him in some form of group ministry. Brandon was comfortable talking one-on-one with people, but his heart seemed to be more uplifted in a crowd. Jake was the opposite. Crowds were to be avoided for the most part. Church attending was the main exception, but then he could just sit back and take things in. Jake shared his faith often, but rarely to more than a handful of people at one time. Brandon felt God's leading to group ministry.

Brandon's mind was focused on all that took place during the teen's service. He wondered, "Was the Holy Spirit at work in the hearts of David and Jason?" It couldn't have been just a coincidence that they offered the exact answers to the very prayers on Brandon's heart. The only thing left that would confirm God's plan was to get the approval from the town board. After arriving home Brandon noticed the blinking light on the phone indicating that a message had been left. He pressed the button and listened.

"Hey, Brandon. I talked to a town board member today. Give me a call. Uncle Bob."

Could this be the icing on the cake? Bob left no indication that the board would approve; yet, there was something in his voice that left Brandon feeling hopeful. He acknowledged the message and cleared the buffer. Then he went up to his room and called his uncle.

"Hello, Uncle Bob. I got your message."
"Hi Brandon. Thanks for calling back so soon."
"So what did they say?"
"It's doable."

"There was a moment of silence. The message was loud and clear to Brandon. God wanted him to gather people together around a bonfire on the farm. Brandon thought about his entire life. His father had abandoned him before he even knew who he was, and now they had been reunited and working together. His family had been limited to just his mother, but through her relationship to Aunt Bertha, he had been brought to the farm. The words in Ephesians chapter two echoed in his head. Was this the purpose that God had for him?

"Brandon, are you there? Hello!"

The silence remained for a moment.

"I'm here, Uncle Bob. I think I was having a God moment."
"Yeah! I have those now and then."
"So what does 'doable' mean?"
"I showed my friend, Joe, the sketch that I made of the property and presented your thoughts for a pit. They had a few concerns, but nothing that we can't handle."
"Like what?"
"They liked your drainage idea, but wanted a water source nearby, in case the fire got out of hand."
"Makes sense. The old well water was piped to the barn. Jake and I can tie into that and continue a few hundred feet further back near the pit site."
"The rest of the recommendations involve a ditch and some rules, which we can comply with quite easily."

"So when can we start?"

"I applied for the permit in your name. I will stop by tomorrow evening and drop it off for you to sign."

"That's great news. Before we start, however, I need to break it to my dad. He has a phobia about fires."

"God has led you this far. I am sure that He will work in Jake's heart as well."

"I hope so. At least I trust that He will."

By the way, I want you to know that I am so proud of you. I am sure Aunt Bertha is smiling right now as well."

"Do you think that God shows the future to heaven's dwellers?"

He can do anything. I know that if He wants for you to lead a bonfire ministry, great things will happen."

"Makes you wonder, though."

"I will see you tomorrow with the papers, Brandon."

"Great, Uncle Bob. Thanks for getting back to me so quickly."

"No problem. Bye."

"Bye, Uncle Bob."

As Brandon ended the call, he could hear the rest of the family rustling downstairs. Terry, often, would have a baked treat prepared after the midweek service. As that thought entered his head he darted down the stairs to the kitchen. An apple strudel was sitting on the island ready to be served.

"You're looking pretty chipper, Brandon," Terry said as he entered the kitchen.

"I had a great day. I really enjoyed the teen's service tonight."

"I enjoyed having you there," Alicia added.

"Me too," Diana and Nicole inserted, almost in unison.

"The strudel is still warm. Anyone want a little whipped cream or a scoop of vanilla ice cream?"

"I'll have some of both, Terry. Thanks."

"You got it."

The conversation over the midweek snack usually centered on school activities, but God had a different agenda. Alicia shared about her friend from church who gave her heart to the Lord that evening.

"Lisa prayed to accept Jesus as her lord tonight. She heard Jason's testimony and came forward while the band members were putting their instruments away. I was there to help."

"That's fantastic." Brandon shouted with joy.

"Brandon, Lisa has been coming for about three months. She came from a broken home. We, I mean the teens, have been praying for her to find peace."

"Sounds like she was a troubled child."

"Her father was an alcoholic and often beat her. Her mother wasn't much better. Anyway, after hearing Jason's testimony, she came forward. He had a similar relationship with his father."

"I really enjoyed listening to Jason," Brandon continued.

The rest of the family shared in Alicia's joy. There's something about watching a lost soul saved that overrides all everyday events. No one mentioned how his or her day at school or work went. Jake took a moment to pause from the conversation and prayed aloud for Lisa. Jake's prayer, for God to provide someone to be her mentor and friend, especially moved Brandon. Perhaps, that was on Jake's heart because of those placed in his life that led to his salvation. Lisa had made a bold step, but it was only the first of many. Before the prayer time had ended, Brandon added a prayer for the youth group.

"So, Brandon, how has your day been," Jake inquired.

"It's been great, Dad. Working with you is wonderful, but I think God is calling me to serve in a new way."

"Want to talk about it?"

"I will, when I have a bit more definition. Anyway, that is why I overslept this morning."

"Fine. When you're ready, I would love to hear more."

After everyone else left the room, Terry went over to Brandon and asked:

"Does this have anything to do with our conversation last night?"

"Yes. Uncle Bob called and said the bonfire is a go."

"I sense that you are worried about passing the idea on to Jake."

"Uncle Bob thinks he will come around, but I guess I am waiting for the right moment."

"So what did Uncle Bob say?"

"He's coming over tomorrow with some permit papers. We will need to provide water and he said something about a ditch. Anyway, The town approved the idea."

"God must have plans for it. Everything seems to be working out. Don't worry about Jake. I will talk to him tonight."

"Thanks, Terry."

"Just keep trusting the Lord."

"I will."

THE PROPOSAL

Brandon went to his room early. The events of the day were heavy on his heart. He prayed for God's wisdom and quickly fell asleep. Jake proceeded down to the living room to read for a while. After Terry made her rounds with the children, she joined him.

"How was work today?"

"Pretty average, Honey. That's not a bad thing. We have work lined up for at least two months steady."

"That's great. Brandon really enjoys working with you."

"Yeah! I enjoy working with him as well. He has a great attitude and shares my values as well."

"God reunited you two for a reason. Perhaps, it is more than just work."

"I think about that a lot. I abandoned him before he was even a year old. He never knew me; and yet, we have a relationship today that is as if we have always known each other. It's so strange."

"God works in mysterious ways."

"That He does. Speaking about mysterious, do you know anything about Brandon's call to serve which he mentioned earlier?"

"Brandon was a bit leery about sharing it with you."

"Why is he hesitant? I'm not sure I understand."

"You will when I share his calling with you. Sometimes, God calls us to do things that we don't understand at the time."

"You mean like Noah?"

"Building an ark in a desert is pretty extreme; yet, Noah was given very specific instructions. Brandon has been called to doing large group ministries."

"That's wonderful, Honey. I prefer small groups, but Brandon does really well with crowds. I still don't understand why he would be apprehensive about sharing that with me. I support him."

"Remember the times when you were a boy and started fires?"

"I remember. I also remember the power high that I felt. Those feelings took me down a dark road before I met you and Christ."

"You are on a whole different kind of high today, Jake Wilson. Christ is your newfound power and strength."

"Along with you, Honey. So where are you going with this?"

Terry paused for a brief moment to reflect. She wanted to have the right words to offer Jake about the bonfire, so she silently prayed for wisdom.

"Have you ever been on a camping trip?"

"You mean like tents and sleeping bags?"

"Yeah! Have you ever roasted marshmallows on a campfire?"

"I remember meeting around a fire with my gang friends, if that's what you mean."

"Do you remember anything about those kids?"

"They were a pretty sorry lot. Most came from broken homes."

"The fire was like a magnet that brought them together in one place."

"I guess you can say that. It also kept us warm on the cold nights in Virginia."

"Brandon's calling involves a sort of campfire. He was not sure what it meant until he talked with Bob."

"He should have talked with me."

"He knew that you had at least two traumatic experiences with fires."

"But that was a long time ago."

Terry left the room for a moment and returned with the sketches of the proposed fire sight.

"Bob petitioned the town for a bonfire site here on the property based on these sketches."

She handed them to Jake and waited for his reaction. The location was pretty clear on the open field behind the barn towards the creek. Terry watched as the wrinkles in Jake's forehead indicated concern. She did not understand at the time what was going through Jake's mind, but felt some relief as she watched him carefully examine each sketch.

"Tell me what you are thinking."

"My first thoughts centered around the fire in the volcano on Hawaii. It started out small and quickly raged out of control. Although it destroyed a large area, I felt a rush."

"Did the thought scare you?"

"The land behind the barn is even more open to the elements than inside that volcano. Yes, I did feel a bit uneasy about it. But, then I examined Brandon's sketches more closely."

"So Jake, what do you think now?"

"I think I need some time to take it in. I think I need to pray about this endeavor. One thing I know, however, is that if God is doing the calling, then I need to trust Him."

"You are truly a wise man, Jake Wilson."

"Brandon is pretty wise, himself. The fires that raged out of control in my life came without preparation. My son envisions a controlled environment with a ditch to prevent the fire from spreading, along with a supply of water to douse it."

"He was pretty worried about how you would react. Pray about it tonight and have a talk with Brandon sometime tomorrow."

"Great advice, Honey. Have I told you lately how much I love you?"

"You tell me often, but tell me again," Terry said with a wink.

Jake pondered the idea of a bonfire. He wondered how God was going to use it to further His kingdom. Perhaps it was a way to unite his family even more. The journey that led him there was filled with God's handiwork. Jake could only wonder about what future blessings might be in God's plans for the Wilson family. The thought of a bonfire resurfaced thoughts of the childhood disasters involving fires. Jake wondered if he would have similar feelings when a fire was lit for the first time. He wondered if he would be afraid for every spark that might float outside the pit.

Terry could sense his restlessness during the night. Jake usually fell asleep and awoke in the same position on the bed, but that night he tossed and turned. She arose early the next morning and went downstairs to start breakfast. Jake came down twenty minutes later and smelled bacon frying.

"Smells great, Honey."

"Are you doing okay? You were pretty restless last night."

"I'm a bit tired, but I'll be fine after I have my coffee."

"Did I hear somebody mention coffee," Brandon said as he raced down the stairs to the kitchen.

"You seem pretty alert. Going to bed early seems to agree with you."

"I slept like a log."

"That's a far cry from yesterday when I had to wake you for work," Jake added.

"I'm ready today. Breakfast sure smells great."

"Working men have to eat. Breakfast is served."

"Brandon, have you any plans after work today?"

"No, Dad. Why do you ask?"

"I would like you to ride with me today."

"No problem."

Terry understood. Jake wanted to discuss the bonfire idea with Brandon. There is something to be said about the bonding that takes place between men when the meeting place is inside a cab of a truck. She felt good and knew that Jake would keep his promise to talk through the bonfire proposal with Brandon.

"Terry shared your calling with me last night, Brandon."

"She said that she would, Dad."

"First, I want you to know that I desire that you always feel comfortable sharing anything with me. My life has had tremendous highs and lows, but my new faith is level ground."

"I appreciate that. I feel called to lead people in groups. The group of teenagers at church has a wonderful group ministry. Jason's testimony last week was especially moving. I hope to lead people to openly share how God has touched their lives."

"We certainly need more of that. So where did the bonfire idea come from?"

"First, it was the hayrides. Alicia, Nicole, Diana, and Matt really looked forward to them, as I did. I heard them discuss the rides with their friends at church. Several of them shared similar times when they were growing up which ended with singing songs around a campfire."

"So that's where the idea came up?"

"Sort of, Dad, but it was more than that. I could see shear joy in their eyes as each child shared their personal memories. They miss the experience. I think our generation is missing that joy as well."

"Perhaps. I reviewed your drawings last night. You covered a lot of my concerns."

"David, the leader of the teen's band, shared some things with me about the group as well. Did you know that someone shares a personal story every week about how Christ has changed his or her life?"

"The girls often remarked about the Wednesday night experience, but I didn't know it was that regular."

"When was the last time that you heard adults share in that way, Dad?"

"It has been a while, certainly not as regular as weekly. I hope that you are not planning to have bonfires every week," Jake said with a look of concern.

When they arrived at the work site, Brandon asked Jake to stay in the cab for a moment. He pulled out the sketches of the bonfire site and began to add more details. Jake not only could sense the excitement in Brandon's voice, but he could see it written on his face. It was contagious.

"This ditch is more like a moat, Dad. I plan on installing drainpipes underground to the creek. In addition to the water used to douse the fire, it will serve to keep the bed relatively dry after long rains."

"Great idea."

"Uncle Bob will help with the trenching. I measured a hundred and sixty feet run from the water tap on the barn to where a faucet can be located to control the fire."

"I can help you with that, Son."

Brandon paused for a moment. Jake had just given his stamp of approval on the project. The seed had been planted. God was at work.

THE MESSAGE

Throughout the day, Brandon paused to write quick thoughts on a three-by-five index card, which he kept in his shirt pocket. He was no longer fearful about how Jake would accept his plans for ministry. Jake was now a partner. The ride home that evening was equally refreshing. The index card held words like: seating, music, events, and times. The pit had not been dug, and yet there was urgency in Brandon's heart to press on. He did not know where the next weeks and months would lead, but he was certain that God was preparing the way. He began dwelling on the possibilities, though final approval might still be months away.

Terry was sitting on the front porch swing, which Brandon had given them as a housewarming present. It was one of her favorite places to be, especially on warm nights. Jake pulled in and the two men walked towards her. She knew immediately that all fears were gone. Brandon's smile said it all.

"Sure is a great day, Terry," Brandon shouted.

"You guys are sure in a great mood. You must have had a good day at work."

"Work was okay," Jake replied, *"but it's great to be home."*

"Did you miss me, Jake Wilson?" Terry said with a twinkle in her eye.

"I always miss you, Honey. I love my family."

Terry smiled as she caught Jake glancing over to Brandon with a quick wink. Body language is such a powerful tool, especially to many women. Terry had several thoughts about the discussion the night before. She hoped that Jake would not dash Brandon's hopes, and the wink confirmed just the opposite.

"You boys hungry?"

"You bet," Brandon responded. *"What's for dinner?"*

"Beef stew. The crock-pot has been going all day. I also made some cornbread."

"You just turned a good day into a great day," Jake said as he warmly embraced his wife.

Dinner was served. Alicia shared about a new friend that she made in school. Matt was excited about getting an "A" on a math test. Nicole was worried about a test she was having the next day in geometry, while Diana shared about a substitute teacher in her English class. The prayer for the food was filled with the concerns and praises of each child as well. The subject of the bonfire was not brought up. Jake agreed to let Brandon bring it up when he was ready. Dinner at the Wilson's was an uplifting time. Jake could only wish that his childhood memories were as good. Nevertheless, he was determined to work together with Terry to ensure that each member of their family built warm memories around the dinner table.

Brandon took everything in like a sponge. Listening to everyone share was music to his ears. He heard it in the Wednesday night teen's group and enjoyed it there in the home every night. Those in his family were quite free to share. How could he promote the same atmosphere around a campfire? People needed to hear that others have gone through similar events and came out better. The everyday experiences of others can have a profound impact on those going through similar things today. Many people hold their feelings inside and maintain a far less optimistic outlook. He did not have all of the answers, but in a small way, he could see the benefits manifested in his family.

By the time Sunday morning came, Brandon had filled his index card with words describing additional needs for his group ministry. Each night he pulled the card from his shirt pocket and laid it on his dresser. Then he prayed for God to provide the answers and direction. As the family headed off to church, Brandon was expectant that God would meet him there.

Upon arrival, the children headed off to their respective classes. Terry went behind the counter in the coffee area to help prepare the baked goods while Jake followed to enjoy a quick cup. Brandon spotted the youth leader, and gave him a shout.

"David, can I share something with you for a moment?"

"Sure, Brandon. What's up?"

"I think God wants me to lead a group ministry at my home. I don't have all the details yet."

"You will my friend. God will provide. You can count on that."

"I know. If He wants me to do something, then He will open all the doors necessary."

"So, how can I help?"

"Well, for some odd reason, I think the ministry involves hayrides, bonfires, music, and sharing. Your youth group is good at the music and sharing part."

"Thank you for the compliment. These kids love both so it's not hard to motivate them."

"I would like to be a part of your group and observe, if that's all right with you?"

"Anytime. You are welcome anytime. Is that all?"

"The town has given initial approval for a bonfire sight on the Wilson property."

"See, God is already at work."

"Yeah! I was a bit apprehensive about how my dad would accept that, but he is on board fully."

"So, Brandon, when do you want to start? The kids in my group would love to help clear away brush or anything else."

David's words came as an initial shock to Brandon. He wanted to inquire about the music aspect. He thought of asking David if he would lead in the singing, prepare some form of songbooks, or whatever else was required to worship around a fire with praiseful song. The idea of involving the kids in the construction of the fire pit had not occurred to him.

"Nicole, Alicia, and Diana will be helping, but it would be great to see them working with their friends. I must confess that I did not think of asking you for support in that way."

"One thing that I have learned in life is that if you take ownership in something, then the experience is heightened."

"Like my first car?"

"What do you mean?"

"I saved for over a year, working odd jobs. I finally was able to purchase a ten-year-old Mustang. It needed a lot of bodywork, but the engine purred."

"Sounds like a clunker that I owned."

"It was mine. I loved that car. I repaired the body over a six or seven month period. When I was finished, I felt good about all that I had accomplished."

"Did you have help?"

"Some of my friends pitched in from time-to-time. When the engine started to misfire, Jerry and I rebuilt it as well."

"Jerry?"

"He was a kid from high school who loved to work on cars. He was a wiz on engines."

"So how did you meet Jerry? Do you remember?"

"I met him in the school parking lot after classes were over. He heard my car making a less than pleasant sound and came over to help."

"Looking back, do you think Jerry was sent by God?"

"I didn't back then, but Jerry did meet my needs. I couldn't afford a new engine, and I knew it was a matter of time when the misfiring would become worse."

"When we are in the middle of a crisis, we don't often recognize God's handiwork. Have you seen Jerry lately?"

"Now that you mention it, no, I haven't. In fact, that summer his family moved out of state."

"That's proof my friend."

"What do you mean?"

"Jerry was your answer to prayer. I bet that you can look back on many times in your life when people crossed your path for only a moment and made a difference. God sees the whole picture."

Brandon paused to think about those words. The very fact that he had been reunited with his father added significance to the fact that God has control of the big picture. He wondered what ever happened to Jerry. Jerry had a talent to work on cars, and he was used to do just that for him a few short years ago. Brandon wondered about what talents he had and how would God use them. Jerry also had a servant's heart. He offered to help a stranger by hearing the sound of a poorly running engine. He never asked for anything in return. He, simply, enjoyed doing the work. Brandon enjoyed working with wood. It was this skill that brought him face-to-face with his father during the repairs on the old farmhouse.

Before Brandon could discuss his need for a music director for the meetings around the bonfire, David dismissed himself to lead the youth group. Still, the conversation left Brandon with more to think about. If God placed Jerry in his life at just the right time, then surely, He would provide others in a timely fashion as well. Brandon was comforted by the thought. From that time forward, he kept his antennae high as if to question whether each new face was a messenger from God.

The youth group praised the Lord in song and testimony as it did before. Hymns were sung without books or overhead projection screens. Brandon did not know the words, yet, he found himself learning the choruses pretty quickly. He was impressed by how quickly the teenagers moved from a high-energy praise song to a soulful hymn like, "How Great Thou Art." The last verse was sung without music, and everyone was unified. Brandon entertained thoughts of a moonlit fire concluding with a song like that. These kids got it. They knew that life was not a roll-of-the-dice. They knew Jesus, and that all things were possible through Him.

Brandon stood for a while in the back of the room and watched each child as they exited the room. There was a lot of hugging, wide smiles, and joy. They were like a big happy family. No one was left out, even if someone was there for the first time. The sight was heartwarming and encouraging. Brandon desired that kind of atmosphere in the group ministry that he would lead. He wondered if the youth would be used as a catalyst for adults to openly share with each other in like manner.

He came to that church with great expectancy and was not disappointed. Perhaps David's words were part of God's plan. Full of anticipation, he joined Terry and Jake in the sanctuary for the morning service. After sitting down, Brandon opened the bulletin to review the various scheduled events. Summer was nearly over and many small groups were being offered. For the most part, these groups focused on people with common interests like young mothers or adult Bible studies. Sharing with others having similar backgrounds or interests is good, but God seemed to be leading Brandon towards a ministry involving all ages. As he read through the list, he envisioned a future flier to involve families enjoying hayrides, roasting marshmallows, singing, sharing, and laughing around the warmth of a fire.

The sermon title was "Trust and Obey." The message was not a new one. Brandon learned long ago that the secret of a fulfilled life in Jesus was faith, trust, and obedience. He felt God's call on his life and was ready to carry on his mission. Though the index card held many unknown pieces, Brandon trusted

God completely for the answers. Prior to the message, the old hymn was song with the words:

"Trust and obey. For there's no other way. To be happy in Jesus is to trust and obey."

Following the song, the pastor began with the words:

"Are you trusting Jesus?"

The question was personal. Brandon wanted to please the Lord by completing the tasks that he was being called to accomplish. Yet, he wondered whether he was truly trusting Jesus. The index card had so many unknowns. He thought that David would be the one who could be recruited to lead the music, but somehow the planned conversation took a different turn. Brandon felt uncertain about the answer to the question and was drawn to hear more.

"Today, we will look into the lives of two of the most influential men in Biblical history, namely, Abraham and Moses. Hebrews lifts up one man as a man of faith, while the other came up a bit short."

Brandon was very familiar with both patriarchs. He thought about Abraham as a man promised to be the father of many, although his wife, Sarah, was barren and beyond childbearing years. Moses led his people out of Egyptian bondage, stood before God at the burning bush, and parted the Red Sea. Moses wanted God to choose someone else to be God's servant. Abraham tried to take matters in his own hands by having a child through one of the members of his concubine. The pastor's words stirred these and other thoughts in Brandon's head. He listened intently to see where the message would lead.

"Moses was singled out by God to restore his people, the Israelites, to the Promise Land. For four hundred years they had been held in bondage in Egypt. The time was right for them to be freed. Exodus details a chronological account of the life of Moses, beginning with how his life was spared from Pharaoh's edict to have infant Israelite boys killed. Moses was raised in the luxury of the palace as Pharaoh's

son. After killing an Egyptian, Moses fled to Midian where he lived as a shepherd. At the right time, he was called to a mountain, where God spoke through a burning bush. Most of us know that story well."

Brandon pictured Charlton Heston coming down from the mountain carrying the Ten Commandments, with a radiant glow, as only Hollywood could create.

"The rest of the book of Exodus describes in great detail how God was with Moses. To this day the Israelites recognize Moses as a highly esteemed leader. Yet, Moses was not one of the men of faith mentioned in the New Testament book of Hebrews. For most of his life, Moses trusted and obeyed God, but we will see that something happened later, where he was disobedient and never entered the Promised Land."

"Abraham was given a promise by God in Genesis chapter 15 to be the father of nations. His offspring would exceed the number of stars in the heavens. His wife, Sarah, was beyond childbearing years, so Abraham laughed. Yet, the account tells us that Abraham believed the Lord. One chapter later we read about his affair with a handmaiden named Hagar and the birth of his son, Ishmael. Where did Abraham's faith go?"

Brandon was well aware of Abraham's story.

"God did not stop there. Despite the fact that Abraham acted impulsively, God's plan to make Abraham the father of nations was still alive. Though well up in childbearing years, Sarah gave birth to a son. They called him, Isaac, which means laughter. Let's read the account together in Genesis chapter 21, verses 1 through 7."

Brandon opened his Bible and read silently along.

"Now turn with me to the very next chapter and we read these words in verse 2:

² Then God said, 'Take your son, your only son, Isaac, whom you love, and go to the region of Moriah. Sacrifice him there as a burnt offering on one of the mountains I will tell you about.'

First, God acknowledged Isaac as Abraham's ONLY son. Second, He let Abraham know that He saw the love of a father towards his son. Third, He commanded Abraham to go to a place and offer Isaac as a sacrifice on an altar. Finally, God said that He would lead Abraham to the exact place where this would happen. God was testing the faith of Abraham. Abraham did all that he was commanded to do. Genesis 22"10 tells us that he raised the knife above Isaac and was ready to complete the task. As a father, I cannot imagine what was going through Abraham's mind."

Brandon tried to visualize his father, Jake, over him with a knife raised. The picture seemed so ludicrous. Jake would have taken his own life before harming any of his children. Then the pastor read Genesis 22:12.

¹² "Do not lay a hand on the boy," he said. "Do not do anything to him. Now I know that you fear God, because you have not withheld from me your son, your only son."

"At that moment, Abraham became righteous and faithful again. He passed the test and was placed on the wall of faith in Hebrews. Now let us look at the man, Moses. After leading the people out of Egypt, through the parting of the Red Sea, the Israelites began their complaining. They were afraid that they would perish from thirst in the desert. Exodus 17:6 give us these words:

⁶ I will stand there before you by the rock at Horeb. Strike the rock, and water will come out of it for the people to drink." So Moses did this in the sight of the elders of Israel.

"Moses struck the rock with his staff as commanded and water flowed out. Forty years later, they were about to enter the Promised

Land, and the people were complaining about the lack of water. Numbers 20:8 give us this account."

"Take the staff, and you and your brother Aaron gather the assembly together. **Speak** *to that rock before their eyes and it will pour out its water. You will bring water out of the rock for the community so they and their livestock can drink."*

"God commanded Moses to SPEAK to the rock and water would gush forth. Earlier in the chapter we read about Moses' lack of compassion for his people. They were wearing on him with forty years of complaints. Then we read:"

⁹ So Moses took the staff from the LORD's presence, just as he commanded him.

¹⁰ He and Aaron gathered the assembly together in front of the rock and Moses said to them, "Listen, you rebels, must we bring you water out of this rock?"

¹¹ Then Moses raised his arm and **struck** *the rock* **twice** *with his staff. Water gushed out, and the community and their livestock drank.*

"We might call it frustration, as Moses struck the rock with his staff not once, but twice. In that moment, he was disobedient. The commandment was clear. All he needed to do was speak and the miracle of water would flow. Forty years earlier he struck a rock once. Somehow, if it worked before with a single strike, then two strikes would add his personal emphasis. The water still gushed forth, as God was sympathetic to the people, but Moses' would not see the Promised Land. Trusting and obeying is a lifelong commitment. In verse 12 we read:"

¹² But the LORD said to Moses and Aaron, "Because you did not trust in me enough to honor me as holy in the sight of the Israelites, you will not bring this community into the land I give them.*"*

"Even today, Moses is a revered name in Jewish culture, yet he came up short on the wall of faith and obedience. Each of us who accept God's free gift of His son, Jesus by faith must live in obedience. God sent his spirit to dwell in each of us. Listen to the Spirit and trust. Remember, God sees the bigger picture."

The sermon left a powerful message, which Brandon would replay over and over in the coming weeks. If Brandon was to have a place of leadership over a group ministry, then he needed to trust that all things would work out. Suddenly, the index card held far less significance. The sermon had an impact of Jake as well.

Brandon felt the strong call from God to lead a group ministry. He wanted to serve, but he also desired to get everything right. Often people don't get started because they seek perfection. Fear of falling short is very real. Especially when God is concerned. Brandon needed to learn that God is in control. He desires our availability far more than our ability. The message was loud and clear. Trust and obey. Before leaving the sanctuary, Brandon pulled out the index card and prayed:

"Lord Jesus. I lift the concerns written on this card to you and I trust that you will provide everything needed to carry out your ministry. I believe in you. Thank you in advance as I eagerly await your leading."

BREAKING GROUND

D avid ran to meet Brandon following the service.

"So Brandon, when do want to get started?"

"What do you mean?"

"With the pit. I can have the teens help, especially on the weekends."

"I came with more questions about who would do what and had not given as much thought about when to break ground. I guess I wanted the questions answered first."

"God doesn't work that way. Remember the message? Abraham was about to slay his son, and God provided a ram at the last minute."

"You're right, David. Uncle Bob said he would help with his dozer. Once that is done, we need to prepare framework for the cement base. I could use help then."

"Great! Contact your uncle this week and let me know what he says. I think a bonfire is a great idea."

Brandon left the church with a new perspective. He knew that the ground needed to be prepared for the fire pit and began to focus on that alone. All of his questions would be answered in due time. He was sure of that. If God were calling him to a ministry then He would provide everything needed. On the ride home in the family van, Brandon shared about how the message touched him. As he shared, Jake listened intently. It was as though they were on the same page.

"I am more like Moses than Abraham," Jake inserted.

"What do you mean?"

"First, I could never have raised a knife over any child of mine. My faith is not that strong. Second, I get pretty frustrated when things don't go as planned. I can empathize with Moses."

"You have tremendous patience with your family, Dad," Brandon said. *"Besides, much of your frustration comes from your life before Christ."*

"You may be right, Son. I used to be a lot worse."

Terry reached over and tapped her husband's leg as if to say that he was doing a great job in the patience department. The touch was confirmation to Jake.

"I don't know what Christ wants me to do," Jake said with some concern on his face. *"I know that He has led me this far, however."*

"You will know, Dad," Brandon added. *"I cannot tell you if it will come as a wee small voice or a crack across your head, but God will reveal His plan for you, Jake Wilson."*

"Perhaps, He already has." Terry said with a smile. *"You are a great provider, husband, and father. You are God's answer for me. I love you."*

"I feel the same way about you, Honey. I want Him to use me to reach others as well."

"We may never see how our actions affect those we meet," Brandon added. *"We can trust that as long as we live to serve Christ, He will use us."*

"You are right, Brandon. I am happy that you feel called to ministry. Perhaps, I am being called to serve along side you."

"Perhaps you are, Dad. Time will tell."

When they arrived at the house, Brandon took a walk behind the barn where the pit would be placed. He paused and prayed for God's intervention. As he walked back towards the house, he heard a familiar truck sound coming up the driveway. Bob pulled up to the house and Brandon met him.

"Great to see you, Uncle Bob."

"Great to see you, too, Brandon. I wanted to fire up old Betsy. She needs some runtime."

"I'm sure mom has prepared extra food. You must come on in and have lunch with us, first."

"I was hoping you might say that. It's such a treat to taste Terry's cooking, especially here at the farm."

"I'll let her know that you are here."

Brandon entered the house and the aroma made his mouth water. Terry was completing a few tasks while the rest of the family waited eagerly in the living room.

"We need to set an extra place. Uncle Bob is here. I invited him in for lunch. I hope you don't mind."

"There's plenty and he is always welcome here."

"Hi Terry," Bob said as he came into the kitchen. *"Sure smells good. I hope I am not imposing."*

"The crock pot has been going all morning and the biscuits are about ready. Have a seat in the living room. Lunch will be served in five minutes."

"Thank you, Terry."

The mention of freshly baked biscuits made Bob's mouth water. Terry was known for great stews and soups, which added to the anticipation. Bob greeted Jake in the living room and sat down next to Brandon.

"So Brandon, how was church today?"

"It was great. I especially enjoyed the message, Uncle Bob."

"I attended the small Baptist church near my home," Uncle Bob continued in an effort to make small talk. The pleasant aroma from the kitchen seemed to be a distraction. *"The message there was on faith and works."*

"Ours was on trusting and obeying. I guess these are pretty common themes for many sermons, huh?"

"We need to live by faith. That's for sure."

"David leads the teens on Wednesday nights. Anyway, I discussed the fire pit idea with him, and he wants to know when the teens can come and help. I thought of you, Uncle Bob. Is the equipment offer still on the table?"

"You bet. I can load it up this Friday after work and bring it over. If you have everything laid out, we can dig Saturday morning."

"That would be great. I need to get some water and drainage tubing delivered, but Saturday would be fine."

"Count me in as well," Jake added.

Terry called everyone in for lunch. Steam appeared to be rising from the tall platter of biscuits. Brandon offered the prayer and also thanked God for the added guest. The conversation in the living room lasted only a few minutes, but reconfirmed Brandon's call to serve. During the week, he would stake out the areas that needed trenching, along with the hole for the pit. Weather permitting, this time next week; it would be ready for framing the cement pad. Brandon began the day wondering about the aspects of having a successful group service and, suddenly, the project was underway.

Much of the conversation around the table involved the pit. Nicole, Alicia, Diana and Matt were excited about the plans. The idea of having hayrides with their friends added to the excitement. They could see the joy on Brandon's face as he shared as well. Throughout the week they would be sharing with their friends from school.

By Wednesday the piping components had been delivered and stored in the barn. Brandon had three-foot high stakes with colored flags outlining the pit and rows of stakes with white flags marking the trenches for the water line and drainpipes. The water line started by the barn near the faucet and stopped at the edge of the pit. The drain line trench ran from the back of the pit all the way to the creek about a hundred feet away. Truckloads of sand and gravel were to be delivered on Saturday afternoon, with the hope that the dozer work would be completed before their arrival. Everything seemed to be going smoothly. Jake may have had some concern about the cost of supplies, but Brandon insisted that he had it covered.

Wednesday night's service added to the excitement. Brandon attended the teen's worship, only the room seemed to fill up more than usual. There were several new faces, yet everyone appeared to know each other. Brandon stood near the back wall as all of the regular seats were filled. The praise songs began and the sound could be heard outside the closed doors.

As usual, a time of sharing testimonies hushed the crowd. Julie came up on the stage. She was a short blonde-haired girl wearing a loosely fitted top over her jeans. She had a pretty face, but was far from petite. Julie began to speak and everyone was silent.

"I wanted to share my story with you because of a friend who invited me to come tonight. I have felt ridicule from many students in my school due to my weight problem. But, one student saw me as a real person. She wanted to be my friend, and we have been friends for about a week now since school started. She invited me to come here tonight because I accepted Christ as my Savior yesterday after school. I dreaded attending school this year. My family just moved here and my last grade was, well a nightmare. I expected the worst again until Alicia Wilson befriended me."

Brandon's jaw seemed to drop. He was filled with pride as his sister's name was mentioned. The other teens gave a moment of ovation for Alicia as well. Alicia was not bound by stereotypical responses. Alicia saw Julie as God did and followed the Spirit's leading to befriend her. Brandon felt that this night was to be special indeed, and he was not disappointed. Julie continued:

"Alicia came to school on Monday all excited about some plans for a ministry at her house. It was contagious. Everyone she met that day felt the joy that she felt. I was one of them, but I kept it to myself. That afternoon, as I was leaving to catch the bus home, Alicia called out my name. 'Julie' she said. I did not turn around immediately so she shouted even louder, 'Julie.' I turned to see her running towards me. We had only known each other a few days, yet she was running to me. It was a scene that is etched in my mind and heart.

'What is it, Alicia?' I asked.

'God loves you.'

Three little words, but what a difference they made to me. We talked for a brief time before boarding different busses to go home. I remember Alicia telling me that those words were what God commanded her to share at that time. The next day, I was excited to go to school. My mom wondered if I was high on something, as it was not like me to be that eager to attend school. I simply told her that I made a true friend. After school, I waited for Alicia. I wanted to know how I could receive words like that from God. I guess I believed in a Creator, but I had not understood just how much I was loved. Alicia shared how Christ came, suffered, and died for me out of love.

I come to you tonight because of that love. I asked Jesus to forgive me of my past sins and to enter my heart. Thank you, Alicia for being my friend and for sharing those three words with me this week. I love you."

Tears streamed down Brandon's face. As he looked around the room, he could see that tears of joy were everywhere. It was almost as if everyone in the room was being given a giant hug from Christ Himself. Then again, maybe that was exactly what was happening. Alicia trusted and obeyed her Savior. As a result at least one lost soul was saved. Perhaps, Julie's sharing made a difference to others in the room as well. Then David took the stage to lead in song.

"Thank you so much for sharing, Julie. God truly loves you. He loves each one of us, so much so that He was willing to die for us. But God did not stop there. He raised Jesus from the grave. We serve a risen Savior. Jesus is alive.

The session closed with a hymn and one by one each teenager approached Julie with a warm embrace. For Brandon it was a magical moment. Julie could not hold back her tears of joy. She was accepted and loved as a child of God. When the crowd cleared, Brandon made his way down to greet her as well.

"Welcome into the family of God, Julie. My name is Brandon and I am Alicia's big brother."

Julie's eyes seemed to sparkle as she placed her arms around Brandon. Brandon could feel the joy in her heart as she embraced him.

"I have never met anyone like Alicia before. She saw me as a real person. I love her so much."
"She's special to me as well, Julie. I'm sure you two will be friends for a long time."
"I feel that way as well."
"I will, probably, see you at the house in the future."
"I hope so, too."
"Remember to trust and obey Christ every day. Do you have a Bible?"
"I do. Alicia gave one to me."

The two parted and Brandon reflected on all that just happened. A soul was won to the Lord because his sister reached out in obedience to the Holy Spirit. He felt led to use the words, "Trust and obey," in greeting Julia. He wondered if those words had even higher significance in his own life. The sermon a few days earlier changed his direction. The groundwork would be laid on Saturday for the pit. It was as if those words were a part of God's master plan. Whatever it was, Brandon knew that he needed to lean on the Lord continuously.

"Hey, Brandon," David shouted as he spotted Brandon leaving the room.

"Hey, yourself, David."

"I wanted to ask you about the digging. When do you plan to start?"

"My uncle and I will begin Saturday morning. If everything works out, we should be done before the day ends."

"That's terrific. I mentioned the idea to my family, and my dad wants to offer his services."

"What does your dad do?"

"He's an electrical contractor. He wants to donate some pole lighting."

"I never thought of that. We will light the fire at night so some lighting would help, huh?"

"My dad thought you might need lighting and some outlets. I mentioned the idea of using some of the instruments and amplifiers around the fire."

"I wrote down many things that needed to be considered for this ministry, but those were not on the list."

"So my dad can help?"

"Sure he can. Have him stop out between now and Saturday to see the layout. You come, too."

"I'm sure we will. Don't worry about the costs. My dad said that he would supply the electrical components"

"Great! I hope to see you soon and tell your dad thanks for me."

"I will."

Things were coming together at a rapid rate. Brandon knew that God had everything under control. All he needed to do was trust. On the way out of the church, Brandon pulled the index card from his pocket and tossed it into a trash container.

David and his father drove up to the house the following evening. The barn had a new electrical service, which could easily handle the lighting needs. Brandon walked the site along side them and described the plans in some detail. David's father stepped out of the car and approached Brandon with a beaming smile.

"I must say, Brandon, I'm impressed. This is a perfect spot. David has been excited about being a part of the ministry as well."

"I haven't really asked him to do anything, yet."

"He wants to help with the music, if that's all right with you."

"You did mention that you wanted to ask me to help in that area, remember?"

"I did say that, David, but we never completed the discussion."

"Well, it's completed then. I'm willing to help."

"Great! What do you have in mind?"

"I could put together a collection of praise songs and hymns into a small booklet. I think I can get volunteers to play instruments. I play guitar and banjo."

"That would be wonderful. I can't wait to get started."

"Me, too, Brandon. Me, too."

Saturday came quickly. Bob unloaded the dozer and a trenching machine into the barn the night before and was ready to roll by eight o'clock. David and his dad showed up shortly afterwards. Jake was already making the plumbing alterations at the barn for the new water line. Brandon began carrying lengths of PVC tubing out to the back of the pit for the drain line. Bob began dozing the square pit area piling the topsoil around the edges. It didn't take long for the pit to be dug. Along the outside of the pit was a beveled area for seating. The plan was to add stone to prevent erosion and allow for seating well away from the fire. The weather could not have been more perfect.

Bob completed the dozing work and started digging the trenches. As he started, trucks pulled up with sand and gravel, which was needed to act as a base for the piping in the trenches. David and his father laid the electrical conduit, which they brought on the company truck. Jake ran the water line, while Brandon handled the drainpipes. Bob used the trench machine to carefully place sand and then gravel into the trenches as support for the various pipes. By noon, everything was in place, including the draining tile, which would surround the pit area for water runoff.

Everything was working better than a Swiss watch. Bob had contacted the site inspectors who arrived around one that afternoon. The approvals were given and by four o'clock, the trenches were covered. David's father mixed cement and poured footers for the light pole bases, which could be installed later that week. Each base would include outlets as well. Additional trucks carrying stone arrived while the trenches were being covered which were dumped in small piles around the pit perimeter. By the time Terry called the crew in for dinner, the stone was spread and the pit was ready for framing the cement base.

"How many people can sit around the fire comfortably, Brandon?"

"My guess is between seventy five and a hundred, David."

"I think we can have even more if they sit on the mounds above," Jake added.

"Things sure look great," Brandon blurted. "I can't wait to see God work here!"

"When do you think you will have the first fire?" David's father inquired.

"If I can get the cement poured in a couple of weeks, then we might plan something in October. I don't have an agenda, but I am confident that God does."

"I think it will be pretty soon, Brandon. Look how fast this has come together. You only mentioned the idea to me a little more than a week ago."

"You are right. Things have really escalated since then."

"I plan on completing the lighting and outlets before Wednesday," David's father added.

"Thank you so much for your generosity. With the lighting we can make preparations easier, like setting up folding chairs."

"My pleasure. I may be providing light, but I believe you will be helping people see God's light in this ministry. I am proud to be a part."

Throughout the day, Alicia, Nicole, Matt, and Diana provided drinks and home baked treats for the workers. When the work was completed, they came out to view all that had been accomplished and were amazed. Jake told everyone to be still, and he prayed for the site to be used to glorify God. Others joined in as well.

DENNIS A. MCINTYRE

FINAL PREPARATIONS

After dinner, Bob called Brandon aside to discuss the tasks remaining.

"Brandon, I have some wood forms that we used at the housing site for driveways. Do you think you can use them?"

"Sure, Uncle Bob. I need four ten-foot lengths for the base. I think we can break the area down into four five-by-five foot sections for pouring. I also need some leveling boards."

"I will bring them out after work on Monday."

"Does that mean that the teens can come out on Tuesday to help set them in place," David added.

"Tuesday evening is fine, provided the weather cooperates, but it won't take long to construct the frames."

"These kids, probably, have never done anything like that. It should be a great learning experience for them."

Brandon could not help but think about all the times his uncle paused to show him techniques in the carpentry trade. Setting the frames involved getting the proper angles to allow water to flow towards the drainage area outside. Although, it would take several times longer, he agreed that the teens could help. He would provide the mentoring.

"Tuesday should work out fine, David. Anyone who wants to learn can come out. Let's say around six-thirty."

"I will see many of them tomorrow at church."

"I'll be ready for them on Tuesday."

Bob delivered the framing materials on Monday evening on his way home from the work site. He wasn't disappointed when Terry invited him in for supper as well.

"Can't turn that down, Terry. Thank you."

"Thank you, Bob. I know Brandon appreciates all of your effort."

"Tell him that I do it for the great meals." Bob laughed.

As he spoke, Jake and Brandon arrived.

"Hi, Uncle. Thanks for bringing the forms."

"I loaded an old cement mixer as well. I thought we could mix our own batch. I noticed that you still have a healthy pile of sand left."

"It will take a couple of yards. Can that mixer handle that much?"

"You may have to build the base in smaller sections, but it can do it. I used it for my patio which is bigger than your pit."

"I have spread cement before, but only mixed small bags for post holes."

"No problem, Brandon. I'll teach you."

"You've taught me a lot already, Uncle Bob."

"We learn from each other. Isn't that what this ministry is all about?"

Brandon pondered those words for a moment. God called him to lead a group ministry without an agenda. Yet, somehow, he knew that everything would come together at just the right time. He often wondered about how God would use a controlled fire to touch the lives of those around it, but Brandon did not doubt that He would. He was certain that God would inspire hearts to share, much like Julie did a few days before. Perhaps, others would hear and be inspired as well. People would learn from the experiences of others. The thought of that raised a level of excitement in Brandon's heart.

"I think that is exactly what this ministry is all about. I trust that God will provide teachers."

"He surely will. You can count on that."

After dinner, Bob and Brandon unloaded the forms and the mixer. While they were laying them out, Ben Richards, David's dad, pulled up to the barn, ready to complete the electrical work.

"Hi Brandon."

"Hi, Mr. Richards. This is my uncle, Bob."

"Hi, Bob. I saw you earlier, but I guess we never formally were introduced. Just call me Ben. That goes for you, too, Brandon."

"Good to make your acquaintance. So you are here to put up the lighting, huh?"

"That's correct. I will assemble everything on the ground, but I could use some help raising them in place."

"No problem, Ben. Let us know when you are ready."

"Will do."

Prior to laying out the forms, Brandon pounded four stakes into the ground to mark the area. Then he attached string lines to each one. Carefully, he stretched the string to the next stake with a small level attached.

"Hey, Uncle Bob. Pull that end tight to the stake."

"Like that, Brandon."

"That's it, but raise it up until I say 'stop'."

"That's it. Now tie it down right there."

When the string lines were completed, the back and front sections of the form were level while the two sides angled from the barn towards the creek. Bob could see that this would create drainage into the back end of the pit where the water could freely flow out the buried drain line. Bob was amazed as he watched Brandon take charge.

"We need to dig out the high spots and fill in the low ones."

Bob understood and grabbed a shovel. Before long, the ten-by-ten site was ready for the forms. When the outside boards were set in place, Ben called for help with the lighting fixtures.

"I could use both of you to hoist the lights over the base plate so I can bolt them down."

The cement bases, which were poured that Saturday, held metal plates with large bolts facing up. Brandon and Bob raised the first light in place, while Ben tightened the nuts to secure it. Then they repeated the work for the other fixture on the opposite end. The poles stood eighteen to twenty feet high with halogen lights attached. Ben made the remaining electrical connections and applied power. It was nearing sunset, so the lights brightened the site, considerably.

"They look great," Brandon shouted.
"I put a shut off switch by the barn so you can have light while leaving. I also installed photo eyes. If you forget to turn off the switch, the lights will go off automatically."
"I love the lighting. Thanks Mr. Richards. I mean, Ben."
"My pleasure. I think my son hopes to bring a gang of kids out tomorrow to help pour cement. The lighting should help."
"It sure will. I look forward to working with the gang."
"I will tell David."

The lights placed a bright golden light over the entire pit and easily lit the path from the barn.

"Look at that," Brandon said as he pointed towards the creek.
"What do you see," Bob added.

A dead tree had fallen and lodged itself over a branch from another tree. The light cast its golden hue directly on it in the shape of a cross.

"Come with me," Brandon shouted as he ran to the site. *"This is where I was baptized. It's almost eerie, don't you think?"*

"It does look like a cross. I'll give you that," Ben said. *"You will have to share your experience sometime. I think you should make that one of your first priorities with your ministry here."*

"I could do that. Perhaps this is a sign from God. I didn't notice the cross form until the light hit it."

"You may be right. It may be a sign," Bob agreed.

"Looks like an altar," Bob uttered.

Although the only planned sacrifices would be logs and dead tree limbs, Brandon enjoyed the view. The lights provided a new look. They had a warming effect. A very comfortable feeling came over the group as they strolled back.

"We can finish laying the inner forms tomorrow," Bob insisted. *"Besides, I am ready for some sleep."*

"You bet, Uncle. Are you all set, too, Ben?"

"I am. Thanks for letting me make a contribution, Brandon."

"No, thank you. The lights are wonderful."

After the men left, Brandon went to the house to see if Jake was still up. Terry was fussing in the kitchen while Jake was reading.

"Dad, are you busy?"

Jake marked the page and placed the book on an end table. *"What's up?"*

"I want you guys to see the lights."

Terry joined Jake at the door and everyone walked towards the barn. Brandon left the lights on, so they could see the golden glow.

"They're beautiful," Terry yelled.

"What a difference," Jake added. "All this has happened so fast. Surely, God is ready for you to get to work."

"God is going to use this place for something very special, Dad. I can feel it."

"I don't doubt that for a minute, Brandon. It seems like you only mentioned the idea a week or two ago, and you are almost ready to lead."

"It was less than two weeks ago, Dad. God is in a hurry to start something here. Tomorrow, David is bringing some teens to help pour the cement."

"I can help with that as well. I see Bob brought the old mixer. I have eight or ten bags of cement mix in the barn. I can get more if we need it."

"At this point, I don't know what we will need. We will pour small sections, so I can tell more after we get started. Anyway, thanks for your offer to help. I appreciate it. These kids want to learn, and I am not sure that I am the right person to teach them."

"No problem, Son. I have mixed cement before."

Tuesday evening came quickly. Before Brandon completed his dinner, several cars filled with teens pulled up into the yard. Brandon expected one car at best. The idea of playing with cement did not seem to have the same appeal as a water balloon war or a hayride. Five or six turned into over two dozen workers. There were as many girls willing to help as boys. David took the crew to the site while Brandon led the way.

"Looks great, Brandon. My dad said that the lights made a big difference as well."

"They sure did, David. I cannot thank him enough."

"He told me about the cross marking the place where you were baptized as well."

"Let me show you."

Brandon led everyone to the creek. It was still daylight, so the lights were not lit yet.

You'll have to use your imagination a bit. When the lights were turned on, a golden glow appeared right here." Brandon pointed to the fallen tree and the one where it intersected.

"I can picture that," David said with a smile. *"So, how deep is the water here?"*

"It's between three and four feet, except during the rainy season. Then the banks flood and the water is pretty muddy."

"It looks pretty clear now."

"It's like that nine months a year."

While they were talking, a few of the kids took off their shoes and socks to wade. The creek was wide and easily accessible.

"Watch out for the rocks," Brandon shouted.

"The rocks are really smooth," one teen shouted.

"I just don't want anyone to fall and get all wet," Brandon added.

Brandon wanted to begin the mentoring session so he motioned for everyone to put their shoes back on and come to the pit. Jake had made his way down and was preparing the mixture. Brandon outlined the plan to put down the remaining inner forms and mix small batches of cement to fill each section. Steven listened intently and then made a suggestion that changed everything.

"I think we should make this unique. The outside forms are in place, but there are plenty of rocks down at the creek. We could bring them here and make the pad like the one my dad built behind our house."

"So, Steven, how did your dad make it?"

"He washed the stones and laid them into the cement mixture like a mosaic. The surface may not be smooth, but it worked for us."

In an instant, the plans changed. Jake went to fetch the wheelbarrow while the teens ran to the creek to collect rocks. Those who arrived first removed their shoes and socks to get the smooth rocks in the creek bed. Small piles were built on the bank. Others took turns hauling the wheelbarrow loads to the pit. Jake planned to demonstrate how to mix cement, but the teens were like worker bees on a mission. One group connected a hose to the faucet installed at the pit and placed it near the mixer. As the rocks were hauled up, some teens rinsed them while others carried them to the pad. Jake poured a layer of cement near the back of the form while Brandon took the lead in placing the stones.

Steven had watched his dad do this same work before and volunteered to apply the finishing application of cement. Anyone looking on might think that these kids had done this many times before. They were working together as a single unit. As the pad neared completion, those collecting rocks were told to stop. One last task remained.

"First, I want everyone to hold hands around the pit," Brandon insisted. *"Then after we pray for God's blessings on this place, I want everyone to bend down and write their initials in the cement between the rocks. Can you do that? You can use your fingers or a stick if you like."*

The men could hear the water splashing lightly against the rocks. The sound was very peaceful. The pit appeared diamond shaped as they looked back. The golden hue captured the shape and radiated off of the banks above.

Everyone agreed. Then Brandon cut open a handful of burlap bags, which were piled in the barn and had the teens spray them with water. Then they were instructed to cover the pad like a blanket. Brandon told them that it was essential that the cement at the bottom dry before the top. The wet burlap would prolong the drying process for the top.

Before they left, Brandon lightly hosed the burlap down. As he sprayed the lights came on. A small rainbow appeared in the mist. It was as if God was placing His blessing on all that had been accomplished. Once again, Brandon expected one result, and God had a different idea. The rocks from the creek seemed like an altar as they now were permanently imbedded on the pad. Later, Brandon would visit the creek and find a soft sandy floor below. The teens were there to be mentored, but Brandon was the one on the receiving end. God knew what He was doing. Brandon knew to trust in all things. He abandoned his plans for the group and was rewarded. He learned what "synergy" was all about, where no one person's ideas are better than the sum of many.

Terry made fresh chocolate chip cookies and brought them down for everyone to enjoy. Jake shared with her all that took place that evening. She did not see the rocks, which were covered by the burlap, but she knew they were there. The cookies were just the thing to end an evening of joy for the teens. Each child beamed as he or she shared what the experience meant personally. It was something that would be etched in Brandon's heart for some time.

THE PROMOTION

Brandon sat back on the lounge chair in the living room and thought about all that had happened. He couldn't wait until the next day when the burlap would be removed and the finished work was exposed. He wondered how the rocks would look in daylight. He hoped that each child's initials would be clearly seen etched in the cement. With the pit ready, he wondered what event would be next? These and other thoughts kept him occupied well after Jake and Terry retired for the night.

Driving home after work the next evening, Jake passed a business with a large stack of broken pallets piled next to a dumpster. He knew that hardwoods were used in their construction and that they may be good for firewood for the pit. He pulled in to inquire.

"Dad, why are we stopping here," Brandon asked.
"Those broken pallets could be great for firewood, don't you think?"
"I believe they would be, Dad. Good thinking."

A receptionist greeted them as they entered the building.

"Hello. Can I help you?"

65

"Hello. My name is Jake Wilson. I would like to know if the pallets stacked near the trash dumpster are available for burning?"

"You will have to talk to our manager, Bob Edwards. I will page him for you."

"Thank you. I really appreciate it."

"You're welcome. Please have a seat and I will call you when he arrives."

Jake and Brandon reviewed various posters on the waiting area walls. The company appeared to be in the packaging business. The processes were varied, so they reasoned that it manufactured different equipment used in industrial processes. Before they had a chance to sit down, the manager entered.

"Hi. Bob Edwards here. Can I help you?"

"My name is Jake Wilson and this is my son, Brandon. I noticed a large pile of broken pallets stacked outside. I was wondering if we could take them off your hands to burn."

"Take all you want near the dumpster. They are an eyesore and we cannot use them in the plant."

"Thank you, Mr. Edwards."

"You have aroused my curiosity. Can I ask where you plan on burning them?"

"We live on a small farm a few miles north of here. The town has given us permission to have controlled fires in a pit on the property.

"So, Mr. Wilson, how often do you intend to have these fires?" The manager inquired.

"My son, Brandon, is in charge of that detail. It's his event."

"I'm not sure right now, sir," Brandon responded. *"Maybe once or twice a month."*

"Who's your audience, young man?"

"Anyone, I suppose. I am promoting it through my church. All I know is that it will be all ages. I think I will have a high turnout of teenagers, however. Perhaps, their parents will come as well."

"Sounds like a great event. I used to love campfires with my family. Smores were the best. Can you still buy those chocolate covered graham crackers?"

"You sure can."

"Anyway, stop back anytime you see the pallets. I'm glad to get rid of them."

"Thank you, sir. I'm sure they will be a blessing for us."

Brandon and Jake loaded a large stack on the back of the truck and drove home. A place was cleared out behind the barn to stack them. After dinner, Brandon used a chain saw to cut them into smaller pieces. Jake took the truck to get the remaining pallets, which took several trips. Before sundown, about half of the pallets had been cut and stacked.

At one point Brandon took a break and went down to the pit. He removed the burlap and was pleased with what he saw. The surface was pretty flat, despite the mosaic appearance formed by the rocks. Stephen had built up the cement around them so that the smooth rocks barely rose above the surface. Brandon gave the surface a light spray from the water hose and watched the water quickly run off the back. He sighed. No stone looked out of place. To Brandon, it was a beautiful sight.

It was the second week in October. The evenings were beginning to get on the cool side, with temperatures down in the lower fifties. Brandon wondered about the possibility of a hayride and fire before Halloween. Rather than witches and goblins, he thought about praise and worship. The idea of turning a secular holiday into a meaningful experience with God captured Brandon's thoughts. He thought of initiating such a plan through the church, so he made a call to the pastor.

"Hi, Pastor Pete. This is Brandon. Have you got a minute?"

"Sure, Brandon. How's the Wilson family doing?"

"We're doing great. Thanks for asking. My call is about planning a church event."

"What do you have in mind, Son?"

"David Richards and the teens helped construct a large fire pit on the property. The town has approved its use for a bonfire."

"A bonfire?"

"Like a campfire, but a bit larger."

"So how do you intend to use it as a church ministry?"

"All I know is that God wants me to lead a group ministry and the fire is part of it."

"So, you feel called by God?"

"Yes. Things have come together much faster than I could have imagined. Suddenly, I find myself ready to lead, but without an agenda."

"Sometimes, that's the best way to lead, Son."

"What do you mean, pastor?"

"I mean that we often spend way too much time dotting the 'I's' and crossing the 'T's.' Months, or in some cases years, pass without accomplishing anything. We want everything to be perfect."

"I know what you mean. The teens taught me a lot about letting God handle the planning this week."

"That's exactly what I am talking about. If God is in control, who are we to try and work the reins?"

"I called to see what you think about a family night on the Saturday before Halloween. We have a tractor and trailer set up for hayrides, ending with roasting marshmallows around the fire."

"I love the idea, Brandon. I would like to stop out and see the site. Will you be home later this evening?"

"I will."

"Great! I will see you later."

"OK, pastor. I'll let the family know that you are dropping by."

"Make sure Terry knows that it is not for a meal," Pastor Pete insisted with a chuckle.

It was about four that Saturday afternoon, when the pastor arrived. Terry prepared a fresh batch of brownies and chocolate chip cookies in anticipation.

"Welcome, Pastor. It's so great to see you."

"It's great to be here, Terry. The place looks wonderful."

"Thank you. We love it here. God has done some amazing things in our lives, especially by reuniting Jake with his son, Brandon."

"Yeah, Jake shared that with me. I don't think it was a coincidence either. God has great things planned for you and your family. I was so excited when Brandon called today. That's why I am here."

"Brandon's cutting wood behind the barn. Come, I will show you."

Pastor Pete followed Terry to where Jake and Brandon were working. As he arrived, he could see the lighting fixtures and mounds in the back.

"Hi, Jake. Hi, Brandon."

"Great to see you, Pastor," Jake said with a look of surprise.

"Brandon called me this morning with a request, and I told him that I would stop by."

Brandon shook his hand and the three men walked towards the pit. Brandon could not stop talking about all that had happened that week.

"I have grown in the Lord a lot this week," Brandon insisted.

"In what ways," Pastor Pete responded.

"I began by trying to accomplish the tasks that God wanted me to do by my own ability. He does not need my ability, only my availability. I learned that great things happen when I let go of myself and let Him work."

"I wish more people understood that principle, Brandon. Pastors included."

"A week ago I wrote down dozens of things which I felt needed to be address for a group ministry on an index card. Each time I tried

69

to find someone to help with an area, God intervened. Before I knew it, people were coming out of the woodwork. I threw the card away."

"Did you lift up those things in prayer?"

"I did."

"I think God honors your prayers. You desire to do the work that He has called for you to do. Trust Him to do His part."

"You mean like your sermon last Sunday, 'Trust and Obey.'"

"So you were the one who was listening. I knew God meant that message for someone." Pastor Pete smiled.

"I'm sure the words pierced many hearts, Pastor, but you got my attention for sure."

"So tell me about how you intend to use this fire site?"

"Several of the teens shared openly about times they spent with family and friends around campfires. They strummed guitars, sang songs, and told stories. For them, it was a bonding moment in time. I think God wants me to create the same atmosphere here."

"It sure is a great place to gather, plenty of room."

"I think that God brought the Wilson family here. This was where I was reintroduced to my father, Jake, after seventeen years. I never knew him before. Now, it's as if I have always known him."

"Yeah, God has a way of mending broken relationships."

"David Richards agreed to put together song books and help lead the singing. I think I can get people to openly share here at the fire about how God changed their lives."

"People relate well to hearing others share, far more than any message from the pulpit, Brandon. I think that all you have to do is get things started. God will work out the rest."

"So, Pastor, I was thinking about a hayride for the kids, followed by a gathering around the fire. Even the wood has been donated. Families could bring folding chairs, marshmallows, and perhaps, a snack."

"I can have the staff work up a flier for the bulletin. I will mention it from the pulpit tomorrow as well."

"That sounds great, Pastor."

"Now where is that wagon that you plan on using for the hayride?"

"It's in the barn. I will show it to you in a moment. First take a look at the cement slab on the pit"

Brandon carefully pointed out all that happened that Wednesday evening. He could not hold back his emotions as he shared how the teens touched him.

"Each child etched their initials in the cement. Nicole's, Alicia's and Diana's are together over there. Matt placed his on that end. I put the date here."

Brandon's joy was evident as he pointed out each person's place in history. There was something about engravings in cement of carvings on a tree that mark a moment in time to be remembered. He mentioned that David's father donated the lighting. After several minutes of uninterrupted chatter, Brandon shut up and led Pastor Pete to the barn to see the trailer.

"Looks great. I love this barn as well. My grandmother had a farm. I remember many good times playing on the straw."

"Old Betsy is ready to go. My Uncle Bob keeps her in good shape."

"Old Betsy?" Pastor said with a puzzled look on his face.

"She's the tractor. Uncle Bob gave her that name."

"So the tractor is a female?"

"Uncle Bob thinks it is his mate. Don't men name their play things girls name, like say boats?"

"Now that you mention it, I think they do. Anyway, the trailer looks great. How many will it hold?"

"We've had thirty on it already, mostly kids, though. The ride goes around the property's perimeter and along the creek."

"The creek?"

"Oh, I didn't show you the creek. I was baptized with my mom there."

By the time Brandon took his pastor around the property, it was time for dinner. Terry came out to the barn and asked Pastor Pete to join them, which he was more than happy to oblige. Terry's cooking had become a buzzword in the congregation, and it was his first opportunity to taste it for himself outside of baked goods on Sunday mornings at the church. Terry also knew that the pastor lived alone. He lost his wife a few years back to cancer. The Wilson's started attending his church several months later. Home cooked meals were welcomed, especially at someone else's home. Pastor Pete often went out to the same diner in the evening just to get away from the emptiness that he felt in his home.

"Thank you so much for the wonderful meal, Terry. It was heavenly."

"You are so welcome, Pastor. Perhaps, we will see more of you."

"I would like that very much. I am excited about the ministry here as well. Thank you, Brandon, for allowing me to be a part of it. I'm sure we can have everything worked out before Halloween."

"Thank you, pastor." Brandon responded. *"I can't wait to see what God has up his sleeve."*

After sharing with the children, the pastor left. Terry had insisted that he take a sampling of baked treats as well, which Pastor Pete warmly accepted. The next morning the family headed off to church in the van. Brandon was still uplifted by all that transpired that week and asked David if he could share a few words with the teens. David eagerly accepted the offer. The room was full again as Brandon walked up on the platform.

"Hi, Steven. Hello, Julie."

One by one, Brandon called out to each child that he knew by name. He was not a person who remembered names well, but God helped in the recall department on that morning. The kids were astounded, especially David.

"Good morning everyone. Some of you I have not met, but I want you to know that you're all special to me and to God. I want to thank all of those who came out to help at my home this week. The pit is ready for a good marshmallow roast."

Even those who did not make it out to the property knew about the plans. David made the calls and told each teen about the fire.

"The rocks look great and each person's initials came out fine. You guys and gals did a terrific job. You may hear about our first gathering scheduled in a couple of weeks. The Pastor plans on bringing it up during the service. Next week we will have a flier as a reminder as well. I hope you can all come with your families to enjoy a night of fun. We will have hayrides, great food, and a great fire for roasting. Bring your voices as I am counting on you to motivate the adults to sing around the fire. Again, I want to just say 'thanks' for your hard work."

David then shared about how the time spent on the farm was not work at all. It was a labor of love. Many of the teens were still buzzing about the experience. They desired more times together like that so the idea of a hayride had instant support.

Pastor Pete made his announcement as well. The following week's bulletin had the flier inserted. The hayrides would start at seven. Some people volunteered to come early and set up tables for food. The church donated folding chairs, which were set up along the sloped banks outside the pit. David came out during the week to test the sound using his amplifiers. Brandon was trusting God for the agenda.

That Saturday arrived. The weather report called for light clouds and no rain. Jake was relieved as he feared that a caravan of vehicles might do a number on the property. Others wanted to help and were used to direct cars to parking places carefully avoiding the route where the hayride would travel.

Loads of people, both young and old, enjoyed their turns on the wagon. They sang songs, laughed, and truly enjoyed each other's company. As each group unloaded, another eagerly awaited their turn until everyone was satisfied. Many sat and talked around the pit though the fire had not been lit yet. Wood was stacked with kindling in the center of the cement pad. The sun was setting with a brilliant orange glow filling the sky to the west. The light whisper of clouds accented the colors, drawing the crowd to sit and enjoy the sight.

Each family signed a ledger, placed on a table near the pit with their name and how many were in their family. By the time the fire was lit, seventy-four families and over two hundred people were counted. One of the guests arrived late and signed the ledger, "Bob Edwards." Brandon recognized him and made his way over to the table.

"Hi, Mr. Edwards. What brings you here?"

"Call me, Bob. I just wanted to see what all of the hoopla was about."

"It's so great to see you. Those pallets are wonderful."

"Thank you, Brandon, for keeping the plant looking good by taking them away. I have some more things on the truck for you."

"I'll get some volunteers to help." Brandon said, anticipating another load of wood.

"No need. The two of us can handle it," Bob responded. *"I thought you might need some marshmallow sticks that won't burn."*

The two men walked to the truck and removed a metal trashcan filled with steel rods. Each rod had a plastic grip and tapered point, perfect for roasting marshmallows. It was obvious to Brandon, that some time had been spent in their manufacture.

"These look terrific. You must have spent a lot of time making them."

"The tubing was scrap. We have a machine that extrudes the plastic, so it was not as difficult as you might think. I mentioned your

plans to some of the workers and many volunteered to help. I see a few of them here with their families as well."

Brandon was a bit awestruck. He knew that God had been busy recruiting others. The marshmallow holders added a level of safety to the event. Sticks might catch fire. Besides, the holders could be cleaned and reused.

THE FIRE

The pallet wood burned and created perfect coals for roasting. Brandon took charge of monitoring the fire until Jake volunteered to take over.

"Are you sure you want to do this, Dad?"

"I'm sure. This fire is in a far better controlled environment than the ones I remember. I will be just fine. I made this long wrought iron rod to transfer coals from the center of the fire to the extremities so that people can roast near the edge. It's working great."

"I can see that. We can use that for all fires in the future."

"That's the idea."

As the people gathered around the fire, David began playing his guitar. Brandon stood near him on top of the west bank of the pit. The sun's reddish glow was nearly gone, and the glow from the embers intensified. Just as Brandon was about to address the crowd, the pole lights illuminated. David had plugged in an amplifier with a wireless microphone connection and tested it. Then he handed it over to Brandon to begin the festivities around the fire.

"Let there be light," Brandon said with a hint of surprise. "I would like to thank everyone for coming out tonight. Did you enjoy the hayrides?"

The children screamed *"Yeah"* almost in unison, while many adults clapped.

"I would like to give special thanks to Mr. Bob Edwards for the wood and the great marshmallow sticks."

Bob stood and accepted the cheers from the crowd. Then he asked his employees who were there to stand.

"This event has been planned for some time, but not by me," Brandon added and then paused. *"I tried to make preparations after I received a call to minister to groups. The idea of a fire had been firmly implanted in my brain just a few short weeks ago. I never thought that we would be enjoying fellowship so quickly. God has been in control."*

The people yelled, "Praise the Lord" and "alleluia" almost in unison.

"Can I get all of the young people who helped with the pit to stand? These kids hauled the rocks that you see buried in the cement. That was no small task, but I want to tell everyone here that it was a labor of love. These kids taught me a lot about teamwork and following God's leading. Please give them a hand."

After the clapping lessened, Brandon continued,

"Each child's initials have been etched in the cement to commemorate his or her contribution. I am sure that the God of Creation is smiling down as I speak. There are a few more people that I need to give thanks to, and two of them have the name, 'Bob.' I mentioned Bob Edwards earlier. Now, let me ask Bob Richards and my Uncle Bob to stand. Mr. Richards provided the lighting."

Cheers and clapping erupted.

"My uncle helped with the digging as well as drove the tractor for the hayride."

Loud roars came from the children.

"I guess from your response that you enjoyed the ride."

The cheers became louder.

"Does that mean that we should do this again?"

The response was overwhelming. Brandon looked around and saw huge smiles on the faces of parents and children. Some were smeared with chocolate from eating smores, which added to the joy. Brandon took a moment to gather his thoughts as he pondered what he might say next. There was no agenda. Perhaps, this would just be a night of good family fun and fellowship. Yet, he knew that God was leading the event. Silently, he prayed for the wisdom to serve. When he looked up, he saw David handing out songbooks to several teens to distribute.

"It appears that God wants us to sing," Brandon shouted as he handed the microphone over to David for his leadership.

"Let's start with a simple chorus of 'Jesus Loves Me.'"

Families help the younger children with the words, and worshipful singing filled the field. David led them with several rounds of 'Row, Row, Row, Your Boat' and other favorites. Even the musical instruments ceased playing, to allow the sound to magically fill the air. Everyone was participating. The children seemed to be enjoying the moment, while parents looked relieved. Surely, God was at work. Still, Brandon wondered whether there would be sharing of a different kind. Then David took the mike and hushed the crowd.

"First, I want to take a moment to say thanks to Brandon for bringing us all together. Don't worry. We will not be taking up an offering tonight."

A burst of laughter was followed by at least one *"Amen."*

"Brandon came to me to discuss his calling to lead in this way. The fire was placed in his heart to serve the Lord, and he followed God's leading. Please lift your hands with me to say thank you."

The crowd stood. After the applause, David continued:

"Brandon shared something with me this week, after the lights came on for the first time, and it stuck with me. The halogen lights made a glow on a fallen tree over by the creek. It shines against it, as I speak, but not as brilliantly as it did that night. If you look, you can see the cross that the tree made against a neighboring tree."

Many in the crowd recognized the sight and helped others to see it.

"The cross had had an impact, but it meant far more to Brandon as he shared with me. I would like him to share that story with you now. Brandon, would you do that for us?"

Brandon nodded, though he was a bit unsure of what he would say. Once again, he asked for heavenly guidance as he removed the microphone from David's hand.

"Thank you, David, for putting me on the spot," Brandon said in an attempt to lighten the moment.

"I guess the agenda for this party starts with me. First, let me acknowledge my Lord and Savior, Jesus Christ, as the one who will lead me, as I allow His Spirit to speak though me.

Second, when the lights came on last Monday, my eyes were immediately directed towards the trees by the creek. The fallen tree had a golden hue on the horizontal top and again on the trunk of the tree, which held it from falling to the ground. It was a moment that spoke to me, perhaps, like the burning bush to Moses, although not in an audible way."

David paused to gather his emotions, which could be heard in his voice as he shared.

"The cross was a sign that God was in this place and would lead me. I cannot explain the feelings inside me, but I heard God's call to start a ministry for families. I knew it involved a fire and would

be on this land. The rest was up in the air. The pit, the lighting, and everything else here were being blessed. That was the first message to my heart that night."

Once again, Brandon paused. The tree marked the place in the creek where he was baptized with his mother shortly before she died. The farm belonged to his aunt who offered hospitality to them as they had little means of support. Now both women were in Heaven. The emotions of the moment could easily have engulfed him, but he felt a sudden peace like a motherly embrace after a fall. Brandon knew that God desired for him to testify and had prepared the stage for exactly that moment. He looked up, after a brief prayer for guidance, and saw two small rabbits playing near the tree. God was with him, yet he felt the presence of his mother and aunt in that place as well.

"When I was about fifteen, my Aunt Bertha took my mom and me in as her guests in that house." Brandon pointed to the Wilson's home.

"Mom had kept a small apartment for us near here, but her cancer kept her from working as a waitress. While we lived here, we attended church with my aunt and talked about many things. I did not know my dad, as mom was a single parent since I was a baby. We talked about who my dad was and whether I would ever get to meet him. She told me all that she knew, but always said that if God wanted us to be together someday, He would make a way."

Brandon paused again. Tears began to flow down his cheeks. He looked over towards Jake and could see welling in his eyes as well. He moved his lips to say "I love you, Dad," but without sound. Jake understood and returned in kind. Then Brandon continued:

"Mom came to accept Christ as her Savior during her battle with cancer. She would tell me not to worry and that she was at peace with her life. I always knew that she loved me, but I could not understand how a loving God could take both of my parents from me. I held bitterness inside for some time."

The tears began to flow harder and the emotion was magnified in his voice. Perhaps, there were still some things that were not settled inside Brandon, which God needed to bring to fruition. Perhaps, feelings of resentment were still buried in his heart. Brandon thought about these and other things as he gathered himself.

"Mom has been gone now for over two years. Before she left this world, I asked Jesus to come into my heart. I knew that I could not handle all that I was going through, at least not without help. In that moment I asked to be baptized. My mother had not been baptized, and I desired to make it a double dip, so to speak."

A few chuckles could be heard due to the play on words.

"Mom was bedridden and would need help. I asked my pastor if we could do it in the creek behind our house. It was summer. The water was warm and clear. He told me that Jesus was baptized in the Jordan River, which may not have been nearly as clean as the creek. It was on a Sunday afternoon in July. I think the whole church showed up and several people helped carry my mother down to the creek bed where we were baptized. The fallen tree marks the very spot. God made that sign for me this week. For me, it was like an exclamation point that He had something special planned in this place.

A strange silence stilled the crowd. Many of the children were asleep, but for a moment you could hear the water flowing in the creek over a hundred feet away. Brandon may have been prepared for an "Amen" or two, but not for the sudden stillness. Then David reached out to take the microphone.

"I'm sure that there is a lot more to this story, but I want to take this time to offer a prayer for Brandon and everyone here. First, if you have been blessed by his testimony tonight, then I urge you to pray with me. If God has tugged on your heart to be Lord of your life, then come to the tree and accept His free gift of life."

David placed his hand on Brandon's shoulder and paused. Several people made their way to the top of the bank and also placed hands on him. Then David prayed aloud for Brandon, his ministry, and the rest of his family. Afterwards, he took Brandon by the hand and led him down to the creek where the tree had fallen.

"Bring your burdens to the cross. It is a sign of Jesus' arms reaching out to you in love. He is in this place."

When the two men reached the site, several others followed. Bob Edwards was among them. Bob knelt down on the grass in front of the fallen tree and closed his eyes, which were filled with tears. After a moment, Brandon felt led to kneel along side him. He placed his arm across Bob's shoulder and asked if he could pray for him. Bob completed his silent prayer and turned to Brandon. Although Bob's eyes were still red, Brandon could see a glimmer of joy.

"You may pray for me, Brandon. In fact, I would love that. I cannot remember anytime in my life when someone prayed specifically for me."

"Tell me Mr. Edwards, what is on you heart? I would like to pray for something specific for you."

Bob gazed into Brandon's eyes, with a look of amazement. Brandon's request touched Bob's heart. It was a defining moment, which Bob would long remember.

"Young man, when we first met at the plant, I sensed something about you that was different than anything or anyone that I had ever met before. I cannot explain what that was, but I knew that whatever you were planning was for me to witness. That is why I am here."

"God was speaking to you, Mr. Edwards."

"After hearing your testimony, I am certain that He was as well. Your story has remarkable parallels to my life, although I am old enough to be your grandfather."

"I would love to hear about your life, Mr. Edwards."

"Just call me, Bob. Perhaps, we can share together at another time. My story is long."

"Let's do that. I am available most evenings. You can even come over for dinner. You'll love my mom's cooking."

"I'm sure I would, Brandon. I would love that. You asked for something specific to pray for on my behalf."

"Please, tell me."

"Pray for mended relationships in my life. We can share the details later. You have a crowd of people here to be with. Just pray for healing in the broken relationships in my life."

"I will do that. Let's pray."

Brandon took a moment to silently ask God for wisdom. Then he audibly prayed for Bob's needs. The two men rose and embraced. Brandon could feel a sense of joy in Bob's hug, which was a stark change from the tears that he noticed when Bob first knelt. Surely, God had placed the right words in Brandon's mouth, which made the difference. Whatever it was, Brandon was anxious to meet with him at another time.

When they turned back towards the pit, many had gathered their children and helped in the clean up process. Yet, they waited, patiently for Brandon's return. The family time appeared to be a success. One by one, families came up to Brandon to thank him for the wonderful evening. Many children added their heartfelt thanks as well.

"We just gotta do this again," some replied.

"Great smores," could be heard from others.

"Can we keep the songbooks?" Others asked.

After everyone left, Jake and Brandon completed the clean up and doused the fire. They swept the water soaked ashes into the center of the pit to be discarded the next day.

"I think you did a great thing here tonight, Son."

"Thanks, Dad, but God did it. I was just a tool."

"God was certainly in it, but without your obedience, it may not have happened."

"I know that God impacted at least one person here tonight."

"Time will tell, Son. Time will tell."

BOB'S STORY

Brandon shared a small portion of his brief meeting with Bob Edwards with Terry and Jake before retiring for the night. Sunday morning seemed to come quickly to Brandon as he had a very restful sleep. Somehow, all of the festivities of the evening before, which should have left more of a restless night, were replaced with unexplainable calmness. It was as if God had placed His seal of approval on everything. Brandon arose early yet fully alert. The smell of fresh pancakes led him to the kitchen where Terry felt led to prepare a special breakfast before church.

"Smells great, Terry. What's the occasion?"

"I just felt led to make a nice breakfast this morning. I hope you are hungry. If the others don't get up right away, that's okay. They can eat when they are ready."

"I could eat a stack. Thanks."

"So, Brandon. Do you know anything about Mr. Edwards' broken relationships?"

"Not yet. I think we will get together soon for more specifics. My testimony really had an impact on him, however."

"I think you touched a lot of people. I wish more people would share like that. Many people go through life thinking that they are the only ones going through dark times."

"You mean like Bob Edwards?"

"Exactly. I heard others sharing while you were at the creek as well."

"God, surely, knows what He's doing. I trust that He will open hearts to share."

"The fire last night was symbolic in a way, Brandon."

"What do you mean?"

"Fire is often mentioned in the Bible as a method of purging. Perhaps, that is what is happening with Mr. Edwards."

"I see your point, Terry."

Jake came down the stairs as they were talking.

"Smells great, Honey. What are you two talking about?"

"Fire and pancakes, Dad," Brandon quickly responded.

"I'll have a stack. I love your cakes. That was a great fire last night. I must say that I thought I would have those old feelings again, but I did not."

"What feelings?" Brandon asked.

"Fear, power and invincibility. That's what I felt as a child. The fires raged out of control during those times, however."

"Maybe, you didn't have them because everything was in control," Terry added.

"Perhaps, but I sure anticipated them."

"Fire had a different meaning for you back then, Jake. You lived a life without Christ. He has given you the gift of peace."

"You are so right, Terry. You are so right."

The rest of the family made their way down to the breakfast table and enjoyed the food. Each child buzzed about the great time they had around the fire. The kitchen was cleaned, and the Wilson's piled into the van to head off to church.

Upon arrival, Terry headed over to help with the baked goods at the coffee fellowship area. Jake followed while Brandon went to drop off some things in the youth room. After a few minutes, Brandon returned to have a cup of coffee. While he was in line he heard a voice call out his name.

"Brandon, Bob Edwards here."
Brandon quickly turned towards the sound and responded, *"Hi Bob. Can I get you a cup of coffee?"*
"Love one. The blacker the better."
"You got it. Have a seat and save another for me."

Bob sat down at a small table well away from the crowd. After a few minutes, Brandon joined him with the coffee.

"What brings you here, Bob? I haven't seen you in this place before."
"I have been here a few times when my wife was alive, but I haven't frequented a church very regularly since then."
"After the loss of your wife, you should have spent more time in a church. I found the people to be more uplifting and encouraging after mom died."
"That may have worked for you, Brandon, but not for me. My wife committed suicide. I tried going to church for a while, but the people were far less helpful."
"Suicide is a tough thing. I have not known anyone who has gone through that, but the very act must raise a lot more questions than answers."
"You are so right. I asked questions like:
"What could I have done to prevent it?"
"What did I do to cause it?"
"Why did she take her life?"

"Did you get any answers?"

"I felt far more guilt than relief, if that is what you mean."

"So, is that part of your request for prayer for broken relationships?"

"I need to mend my relationship with God for sure, but I have a daughter who holds me responsible for her mother's death."

"That's deep. How old was she when your wife died?"

"Sixteen. She graduated from high school by the skin of her teeth and took off."

"Teenagers are difficult to deal with under normal conditions. I cannot imagine what it was like for her, and for you for that matter. Do you keep in touch at all?"

"I know where she is living if that is what you mean? I send money on occasion which she does not return."

"That's a good sign. At least she is open to accepting that from you."

"I suppose, but I long for her to be my daughter again. I feel that have I lost her."

"I will pray for you both right now. Then I want you to join me with the teen's group. Would you do that for me?"

"I will, Brandon. I would like to talk to you again as well."

"We will."

Brandon prayed for healing in the father-daughter relationship. As he prayed, he could not help but feel remorse. He was the same age as Bob's daughter when his mother died. Yet, she died from natural causes. The idea of suicide left a huge hole to which Brandon could not easily relate. Silently, he asked for the wisdom needed and a measure of empathy for Bob. Then the two men headed to the teen's service, which was already active.

David completed a praise and worship song. Brandon's entry caught his eye.

"How many of you attended the great hayride and bonfire at the Wilson's last night?"

More than half of those in attendance raised their hands. Many of those who were not there had been given first hand accounts from the others. Nearly every face appeared joyful.

"Brandon shared an amazing account which included the salvation of his mother. It, surely, was a great night. I wonder if he would say a few words."

Brandon nodded and began his walk to the stage. Silently, he asked God for the right words to share. He greeted David with a warm embrace and began speaking."

"Last night was far more than I expected, but God deserves the credit."

The audience burst out in praise.

"The only agenda that I had last night was to follow His leading. David put me on the spot to share, but I knew that God was directing him. I know that the words from my mouth were from my Lord even though they reflected my life story."

As Brandon continued, one young man named, Thomas, approached the stage. Thomas was a high school sophomore who kept to himself. He had attended the teen's group for nearly a year, and rarely spoke. Usually, he stood near the back of the room and left as soon as it was over. As he approached, David yelled out his name.

"Thomas, Thomas Wiley. What brings you up here today?"
"I want to let Brandon know that his message had a personal impact on me last night."

Brandon reached out his arms and hugged Thomas. Tears were streaming down the young man's face. Brandon was deeply moved by the emotions in Thomas' voice without knowing what the man had to share.

"I don't know what you are going through, Thomas," Brandon began, *"but God does. You are His child."*

"I started coming to this church after my dad left. I was searching for answers and relief from the pain I felt. I blamed myself for his leaving, though I could not pinpoint anything specific that I did. After he lost his job, he became depressed. I questioned whether I should have been more supportive."

"So, Thomas, what was the message that you heard last night as I spoke?"

"The message was loud and clear. God is in control. That's what I heard. God is in control of everything."

"So, you stopped holding guilt in your heart?"

"I just turned it over to Jesus. I still wonder about my dad as it has been over a year since I last heard from him. But, somehow, I know I will hear from him again. God led you and your father to this place despite unbelievable odds against such a meeting. Your words encouraged me, more than I can express. I desire to be part of your campfire ministry. I sincerely hope that it will continue."

"I don't think God is through with me, yet. Do you live with your mother?"

"I do. Like your mother, she is a waitress."

Brandon paused to reflect. He sensed some of the same feelings in Thomas as he had when his mother was alive.

"What is your dad's name?"
"Alan, Alan Wiley."
"I would like to pray for you and your family right now, if that is okay with you, Thomas?"
"I would like that."

David joined them as they asked for God's healing touch upon Alan, Thomas, and his mother. Bob Edwards found himself praying as well. He desired healing for his family though in a different way. Suicide claimed his wife, but his daughter was lost to him as well. Oh, how he longed to see her again. He wondered if God was in control of his life as He was in the lives of Thomas and Brandon. Before they parted, Brandon assured Thomas that they would talk more in the future. They exchanged phone numbers.

"We will have more hayrides and fires," Brandon said with a smile as he turned to readdress the crowd. "I don't know about the rest of you, but if God is in that place, then I want to be there as well."

The audience agreed with a roar.

"I would consider another event a week from Saturday. I could use volunteers."

Brandon was immediately overwhelmed with support. Teenagers were raising their hands as if they needed to be chosen to help while others simply came forward. The stage was set for a second bonfire. If Uncle Bob could not run Old Betsy then Brandon would for the hayride. The only thing up in the air was the agenda for the evening. Yet, Brandon knew that God would provide.

After the service, Bob invited Brandon to join him for lunch. Brandon sensed God's leading and accepted the invitation. The town diner was known for great soups and burgers so it was a logical choice. Upon arrival, they were seated in a corner booth well away from the entrance, which offered a measure of privacy. Brandon was uncertain as to where the conversation would lead, but felt God's presence and peace.

"So, Bob. How did you like the service today," Brandon began.
"The pastor's message was thought-provoking, but I especially enjoyed the youth class. Thanks for inviting me."

"Those young people are wonderful. I was deeply moved the first time I joined them as well. If they are our future, then we have nothing to worry about."

"If only all teenagers were like them, Brandon. I fear that is not the case, however."

"Yeah! These kids may have many of the same problems as others their age who do not attend a church, but they have a support group here."

"That's great. I wish Angela could find a group like this."

"Angela is your daughter's name?"

"I used to just call her Angel. I still think of her that way although she never wants to hear that name come from my lips again."

"I believe that God will direct your daughter to the right person or group that can provide good council. He does that a lot. Just ask my dad."

"I hope that is true. I hope that she finds her way back into my life."

As they were reviewing the menu, a dark haired waitress approached them. On her uniform was a nametag that read "Lucy."

"Good afternoon, Miss Lucy." Brandon uttered. *"What are your specials today?"*

"I haven't seen you around here young man. Are you new in town?"

"Not really. I come in occasionally during the week for a burger, but rarely on weekends."

"I only work here on weekends. What's your name?"

"I'm Brandon and this is Bob."

"Hi Brandon, Bob. Soup and sandwich items are our most popular. We still serve breakfast items all day as well. Our soups are broccoli cheese, chicken with rice, and loaded potato. We also have chili. Can I get you guys something to drink?"

"*I'll have water with lemon and a cup of decaf coffee,*" Bob replied.

"*Just water for me,*" Brandon added.

"*I'll have a bowl of chicken with rice and a cheeseburger,*" Bob quickly inserted.

"*Sounds good to me as well,*" Brandon added.

"*Coming right up.*"

After Lucy left, Brandon felt led to initiate the conversation.

"*Bob, I would like to know more about your daughter. What was she like before your wife took her life?*"

"*As a child she was a shear delight.*"

Brandon could see a sparkle in Bob's eyes as he spoke. He could sense the joy that was evident in Bob's voice as he related to Angel's early life as a child.

"*Tell me more. What were her favorite things to do?*"

"*Angel loved to chase butterflies. I don't remember her catching many, but there was something about a butterfly that fascinated her. I would run along side her. That girl would wear me out just running.*"

"*She liked doing things outdoors?*"

"*That she did, but she loved helping her mother make cookies, play with Barbie's, and nearly everything else young girls do.*"

"*Sounds like a pretty normal kid to me, Bob.*"

"*That she was. Angel loved going to church as well, especially on Wednesday evenings. She gave her heart to Jesus at the age of eleven.*"

"*That must have been very special for you, Bob.*"

"*You bet. It's also a source of heartache today.*"

"*What do you mean, Bob?*"

"*I fear that she has lost her relationship with God. Leaving me is one thing, but I pray that she stays true to Jesus.*"

"That's a good prayer to have for anyone. I know one thing, namely, God will not abandon her. Even at the age of eleven, I am sure that God honored her choice and dwells with her."

"I pray that you are right."

"So, tell me about her early teenage years."

"Nothing out of the ordinary. She overdid the makeup for a while, but all young girls go through that phase. She was a good student with mostly "A's" and "B's." She had a few questionable friends in school, but we didn't notice any rebellious behavior tendencies."

Just then, Lucy arrived with the soup.

"Burgers will be out shortly. Enjoy."

"Looks good," Bob said with a smile.

"Probably tastes even better," Brandon added. *"I would like to pray for us. Dear Jesus, thank you for bringing Bob and me together at this place today. Bless our time together and this food to our bodies. Provide your hedge of protection around Angela, and messengers to minister to her, wherever she is. Amen."*

"Thank you, Brandon. It is a bit refreshing to hear someone pray like that in a public place."

"I love Jesus. I am not embarrassed by openly praying to Him despite the demands of the world around us. Besides, didn't Jesus warn that even the rocks would cry out if we didn't? The world cannot stop prayer."

"Nevertheless, it is refreshing. Perhaps, I will pray more openly in the future."

"If we are not ashamed of Him, Bob, then He will not be ashamed of us."

"I got the message."

"So tell me about your wife. I know that may be painful, but it also may be therapeutic."

"Angie was a terrific mother and companion until she lost her sister in a car accident. Her sister was not married and a couple of years younger."

"So, the accident changed Angie's life?"

"You can say that. Angie was never the same afterwards. Nothing I could say or do helped to take away her remorse."

"What happened in the accident?"

"JoAnne had just graduated from college and had gone out to the store for a few items. Angie had waited that night for her sister to leave her apartment so she could decorate it for a surprise party. The surprise was a police car with the news that Joanne had been killed instantly by a drunk driver in a head-on collision during her return home."

At that moment Lucy returned with the cheeseburgers. It could not have come at a more intense moment. Brandon was attempting to gather his feelings as he listened to the horror being described the night of the accident. He could see how Bob's wife could feel depression, even to the point of committing suicide. But, there were still more pieces of the puzzle to be put together like: Why would Angel hold her father responsible for her mother's death?

"Need any mustard? Ketchup is on the table."

"I'm fine." Brandon said. Bob just nodded in agreement.

"How's the soup? You don't seem to have eaten much."

"Soup's great," Brandon replied. *"Just waiting for it to cool a bit."*

"Well, enjoy and leave room for a slice of one of our cream pies."

"Thanks."

Brandon wanted to hear more, but insisted that they take time to eat. He ate his soup while thinking about Bob's words. Lucy's interruption seemed to trigger Bob's appetite, at least for a time. Brandon assured him that they would talk more later, but that the burger looked too good to waste. Bob nodded in agreement. After they had finished, Lucy returned to remove the dishes.

"Did you save room for pie, guys?"

"Not me," Bob answered, *"but you could bring a refill of the coffee"*

"I'll take a cup as well," Brandon insisted.

"You got it."

Brandon wanted to get more details into Angie's death and Angel's rebellion. A cup of coffee would ensure that the conversation would continue, at least for a moment.

"So, Bob. Did something else happen the night Angie's sister was killed?"

"Angie was pretty stubborn. I suggested that we have the party at our house and simply invite JoAnne over. Angie insisted that the surprise would have greater impact at her home. She made the call to her sister to tell her that she was going to stop by that night. Angie knew that her sister would go out to buy items for a meal."

"So, Angie felt responsible for her sister leaving the house that evening. If she had not called her, then she would not have been hit by that drunk driver."

"That was a big part of her depression. I think she agonized over that for a long time. She did not sleep for days after the accident."

"Lack of sleep, guilt, and grief can sure spell disaster."

"I could not do or say anything to console Angie. I think Angel blamed me for not being there. I tried everything I knew, but I just couldn't help my wife."

Bob began to weep uncontrollably. Brandon moved to his side of the booth to offer relief. The conversation was well beyond any expectations. The only thing Brandon could do was let him cry. It had been a year since he shared the account with anyone. Yet, there was something in that moment that brought real relief to Bob's heart. Perhaps, he had blamed himself for not doing something. Perhaps, his daughter was right in passing some blame onto her father. Still,

Brandon's presence was heartfelt and comforting. Then Brandon looked up and said:

"Lord Jesus, I pray right now that You provide Your healing touch upon Bob and his daughter, Angela. Bring her back to her father. Unite them as a family and mend the broken hearts. I pray that You will be merciful and restore them even now. Amen."

Bob's tears began to stop and a look of joy came over him. It was as though Brandon's prayer produced a spark of hope that Angela would return.

"I have never had anyone pray like that for me. Thank you, Brandon."

"I believe that God will heal you, Bob."

"Somehow, I believe He will as well. Now lunch is on me."

"Thanks, but I can buy."

"I invited you, so it's on me."

"I will continue to lift you and Angel up daily, Bob."

"You are a messenger from God, Brandon. I truly believe that."

"God uses everyday people all the time, even you."

"You may be right, but today He used you to help me. I know He did."

THE DINER

Upon leaving the diner, Brandon looked over at Lucy and waved. There was something in the exchange that felt a bit eerie. It was as if a new relationship was about to form. He felt God's leading to have the bonfire, and similar feelings came upon him regarding Lucy. Somehow, Brandon knew that Lucy was in God's plans for his life. She was old enough to be his mother so he did not interpret them as anything romantic. Still, he glanced back in her direction after leaving the diner and wondered.

Brandon would revisit the diner on weekends when she worked. Each time, he would ask for her by name when the diner had several waitresses working. Lucy often called him out by name as soon as he entered. When business was slow, she would come over and sit with him. Often, the conversation would cover the normal events, including weather, work, or the news of the day. One Saturday morning was different. It was nearly two months since the first bonfire at the Wilson's. There have been four since. Each one had a growing audience. The diner had fliers posted for the last two events. A new one was posted for the one that evening.

"So, Brandon, are you all set for the festivities tonight?"

"I hope so. It seems as though each night is drawing bigger crowds."

"My son, Tom, has been to every one and is very excited about tonight. He told me to get there early."

"So, Lucy, you plan on coming tonight."

"I have to. My son insists."

"You'll have to introduce me to him. I'm sure he is a fine young man to have you as his mother."

"You have already met him."

The name 'Tom' is pretty popular so Brandon could not put a face with the name.

"I'm sure I have, but I have met many people with the name Tom."

"Just a minute, Brandon. I have a picture in my purse."

Lucy went back behind the counter to retrieve her purse. She returned a moment later with two wallet-sized photos.

"That's Tom running on the high school track team. I took the picture because I thought he looked so cute in his uniform."

Brandon glanced at the picture, but the view was from a distance. The young man had a look of familiarity, but Brandon could not recall. Then Lucy handed him another picture that was from a recent school yearbook photo. Brandon's faced recognized Lucy's son immediately.

"I can't believe it. Tom is your son."

"You say that as if you have known him for a long time."

"I have only known your son for about two months, Lucy, but I feel as though I have known him for a lot longer."

"What do you mean?"

"Tom spoke up at the Sunday morning youth group following my first bonfire."

"Yeah, he told me about that. He went to the hayride to hang with his friends and came back full of excitement."

"Tom shared that he related to the message I shared about my life."

"He talked for hours with me about it as wellI just did not know that the person he related with was you, until now."

"He said his mother worked as a waitress. It all makes sense now."

"What does?"

"When I first met you that Saturday morning with my friend, I felt drawn to you. God does that to me on occasion, and I find myself wondering why."

"Tom told me that you never knew your dad until recently. Is that correct?"

"My dad left when I was a baby. He was pretty wild as an eighteen year old. Fatherhood must have really frightened him. Anyway, God led him back here after he got his life in order. He is a changed man today."

"How so?"

"God has got a hold of him. His father left him when he was about five. He got mixed up in a lot of the wrong things, at least until he met Terry."

"Terry? Is that his wife?"

"Yeah! She's terrific as well. You have to meet them at the bonfire tonight."

"I am looking forward to that. I have a customer, so I have to go. I want to talk more, however."

Brandon was beginning to see a bigger picture, though there were still many gray areas to be enhanced. It was as if his entire life was unfolding in front of him, starting from his birth. The words in Ephesians took hold like they were written especially for him.

Ephesians 2:10 (NIV)

10 For we are God's workmanship, created in Christ Jesus to do good works, which God prepared in advance for us to do.

God was molding Brandon into the man that He wanted him to be. His life was no accident. His father's abandonment was part of a bigger plan. His life's struggles were designed to lead him to this point in his life where he would be used to help others going through similar experiences. The hayrides and bonfires were drawing people in the community together with a measure of excitement. Brandon could only wonder what would unfold next, especially in the lives of Tom and his mother. He pondered what pain might be relieved, or what forgiveness needed to be offered. Nevertheless, Brandon had a warm feeling of comfort knowing that God had been and is in control all along.

Brandon reflected on the events that led his father back to reunite with him after eighteen years. Until that point, Brandon rarely went outside the comfort of his apartment. Uncle Bob insisted from time to time that he join him for a meal or help him at work, but for the most part, Brandon stayed close to home. Since being with his father, the comfort zone has expanded to well beyond the farm. He was a regular attendee in church on Wednesdays and Sundays. Now, the diner had become a welcomed place. Wherever he goes, Brandon had his antennae actively seeking those whom God had in his way. Knowing that He saw the whole picture, gave him confidence, peace, and boldness to expand his sphere of influence well beyond any perceived comfort zone. Not only were Brandon's senses heightened, but also, each day became a new source of excitement. Brandon's thoughts focused on Lucy and Tom as he pondered God's work in his life.

Lucy completed her duties and rejoined Brandon at his booth. Brandon had several thoughts about where to enter the next conversation. Then God placed words in his mouth to utter.

"So, Lucy, I want to hear about Tom's father. Tom shared with me that we had a lot in common. I know that he left when Tom was a teenager so that is different from my dad leaving me as an infant."

"Alan had demons in his life."

"Demons? What kind of demons?"

"He listened to the wrong crowd. He was brought up with the idea that a man's worth was measured in how well he provided for his family. Alan had a great job, working as an engineer in NASA. The downsizing process added him to the unemployed list. Though he had marketable skills, no one was interested in this location."

"So, the next step would have been to look else where. Did he do that?"

"He spent every waking hour afterwards on the internet. First, he tried to stay in the state. Then he moved the boundaries beyond to include the southeast. Still, there was some voice in his head that nagged at him about being a failure to provide for the needs of his family."

"Did you know that Tom blamed himself for his father's leaving?"

"Not at first, but I could sense some form of guilt. Tom had nothing to do with his father's leaving."

"Did you share that with him?"

"I tried. Over and over I tried. It was hard for him to accept that his father left because he felt we needed a better provider. That just did not make sense to Tom."

"So, when did you start waitressing?"

"I took a job at an Italian restaurant in town about three weeks after Alan was let go. I'm not sure whether that was a good thing to do or not. I just wanted to help pay the bills."

"Was Alan receptive to the idea?"

"Not at all. We discussed it at length. He would say that no wife of his would stoop to that level."

"Being a waitress isn't bad. I love interacting with people, especially those who are friendly, like you."

Lucy smiled. A bell rang, indicating customers had entered the front door, so she excused herself from the conversation to serve them. Brandon thought about what it must have been like to lose a job as the primary breadwinner. He had gone months without work, but had only himself to care for so the concept was a bit foreign. Having a wife and child dependent on you would carry additional burdens to be sure, but emphasizing with Alan was difficult. Brandon wondered whether the pressure of working for the aerospace industry enhanced the situation.

Brandon had been in the corner booth of the diner for nearly three hours and the lunch crowd was beginning to pile in. He paid his bill and penned a note for Lucy, expecting to see her later that evening at the bonfire. Then he caught her eye and nodded, while placing the note at the register for her to read. She responded with a nod as if to say she understood.

The hayride would begin in about six hours. Still, the agenda had not been, officially, put together. Like all of the other times before, Brandon relied on God for those details. The firewood was ready with all of the other preparations. The church had delivered an extra batch of chairs for the event and recognized the impact that it had already had on the members.

Brandon's heart was focused on the Wiley family. He could not wait to see what God would do to help them through the trauma in their lives. He could only wonder whether God would lead Tom's father back to him.

COMMUNITY SPIRIT

That evening the vehicles began to arrive in droves. The church bus offered some relief for the parking problems that existed with the much larger crowds. Members were asked to park in the church lot and shuttle over. Other sites in the community offered their resources in a similar way. Uncle Bob had the wagon ready to go, and the first load of families was packed in like sardines. A line of youngsters had already formed along side the barn for their turn on the hay wagon. Parents were smiling and interacting with each other.

Brandon greeted many of the guests as they arrived. Their smiles were contagious as if the activities were part of a long awaited get away like an amusement park. It was obvious to Brandon that hayrides, bonfires, and fun meant a great deal to these families. Whatever was going on in their day-to-day lives seemed to be placed on the back burner for an escape to a small farmland in Florida. The sounds of children laughing added to the joy. Brandon took a moment to pause and lift up the event to his Savior.

"Lord, you have led me to a wonderful place in my life. My heart is full of great joy and excitement for this day. I trust that You will lead as You always have and touch at least one soul for heaven tonight. Guide me and use me. In the holy name of Jesus I pray. Amen."

Lucy and Tom spotted Brandon as the church bus pulled into the yard.

" Hey, Brandon."

Brandon heard his name called and looked around to acknowledge. A moment later, he recognized Lucy exiting the bus and started walking towards her. Tom was following behind.

"Welcome, Lucy. Hi Tom. It's so great to see both of you."
"Looks like you are going to have the largest crowd so far," Tom uttered.
"Yeah! Thank God for the church bus program to get everyone here."
"That's not all," Lucy added.
"What do you mean?"
"Apparently, some of the town's businesses have donated some things to help out. Take a look."

Brandon walked to the rear of the bus where the driver was preparing to open the door. Inside were cases of snack items, sodas, and bottled water.

"I guess this was the town's way of saying 'thank you', Brandon. Customers have come in to the diner asking how they could help. I hope you don't mind."
"Of course not, Lucy. This is fantastic. We tried the 'bring a dish concept' on the first fire, but it was pretty messy. My mom has baked a lot of cookies and we made some large containers of powdered lemonade, but these items are great. When you see your customers, you will have to thank them for me."
"I already have. Now you will need to get some strong-armed men to unload these items."

Brandon yelled to his father to get his help. As Jake approached, he could see the stack of boxes and began soliciting help from the fathers. The bus was unloaded in short order. Brandon marveled at the speed, but even more at the community spirit that existed. The men joyfully pitched in to take on the task as if it was just part of the festivities. It was a teachable moment. What may have looked like a heavy load for one man became light with many hands. The idea that people from the town felt led to donate what they could to help the cause added to the lessons learned.

Brandon started out with a mission to build a fire pit because he felt led by God. He did not think of himself as a leader and had to rely upon the Lord for the skills to lead. He wondered if this was like Moses leading the Israelites, in a smaller scale of course. Still, the moment seemed to etch its way into Brandon's thoughts and added a measure of confidence that he was in God's will. The enthusiasm of the attendees was contagious and heartwarming. Each event in the past provided excitement, but as the crowds came, Brandon's heart filled with even greater anticipation than before. In his wildest dreams, he could not visualize the level of community spirit that was unfolding.

Families moved quickly to the barn to wait in line for their turn to ride the wagon. Ol' Betsy was sure to get a workout. Brandon glanced over towards the barn on several occasions to see children smiling in anxious anticipation of their turn on the straw. Brandon never had the opportunity to visit Disney World even though he lived nearby for much of his life. The joy on the children's faces placed thoughts of what a Disney adventure may have been like. Who would have thought that a tractor and a wagon of straw on a few acres of farmland nestled among several housing developments would produce so much excitement? That was the thought that permeated Brandon's mind.

After everyone had his or her turn to ride the wagon, they began to find places to sit around the fire pit. The seating at the fire level was packed, and safety was Brandon's biggest concern. Additional seating was on the grassy area around the pit with chairs several rows deep. Brandon's pastor was there and made the comment that with such a crowd there should be an offering. He said it with a smirk, however, as the size of the audience rivaled a good Sunday morning service at the church.

"*I am curious, Pastor,*" Brandon began. "*Have you been introduced to new families that may have attended a bonfire in the past few weeks?*"

"*As a matter of fact, I have. I can think of at least five families who have come more than once. I'm sure that number is low, however. You are doing a great thing here.*"

"*Thank you, Pastor, but God gets the credit. I am just following orders.*"

"*You are a great soldier then. God's army needs more men like you and His vision is far better than anything I could have. Have you seen the smiles on those kids as they ride the hay wagon? It's amazing.*"

"*Yeah, and the parents too. Wouldn't it be great if the congregation acted like these families?*"

"*That it would, Brandon. That it would. I venture to say that most of these people were total strangers when they arrived, but they interact as if they have known one another for ages.*"

"*You noticed that, too. Tell me, Pastor. What makes people free to open up like this when their normal tendencies are more reserved?*"

"*Great theological question. Let me answer it with an example. Suppose a hurricane swept though the town tomorrow. How would neighbors respond?*"

"*When the storm passed, they would help each other in any way they could, I suppose.*"

"*That's exactly right. They would have a common purpose and would put away all other less important things to serve each other. God has made us like that.*"

"*I think you are right. Loving your neighbor is often hard to do, but during those times of crisis we see bonds form, if only for a brief time.*"

"*Love God and love your neighbor. Those are the only true commandments that we have. Now we don't have a crisis here, but we have a common purpose. You created that. These people see the occasion as a time of fellowship. The first fire may have brought people out of curiosity, but many of the same people come now as an escape from their everyday woes."*

"Perhaps, Pastor. All I knew when this whole thing started was that I would lead a group ministry."

"That you are doing, Brandon, and doing very well. I'm sure that God is well pleased. Do you have a message planned for the evening?"

"Is that an offer to bring one, Pastor?"

"No. I have enough to do preparing for Sunday."

"I feel the need to share a few things, Pastor, but God will provide the message. He has every time so far."

"That He will do. You can count on that."

Jake had the fire roaring earlier. Now it was down to a glow. The parents took turns helping the children cook marshmallows. Everything was under control. Incidents of children fighting were quickly resolved. Some of the cases unloaded from the bus contained bags of marshmallows and chocolate covered graham crackers from a local grocery store, so no child was denied the opportunity to enjoy a smore or two.

David had the platform set up for the music to begin. It was almost dark and the lights would come on shortly. As he began to tune his guitar, the crowd began to put away the cooking rods and prepare the kids to be still. Brandon looked on the group with amazement. The sound of strumming seemed to trigger a reaction of expectation for what would take place next without any other coaxing. David tested the sound system and made an announcement that the praiseful worship would begin in five minutes. Only a few stragglers needed to find a place to sit in the process.

The worship in music started as David led a few familiar choruses for the audience to join in. He separated the people into three groups and directed rounds of singing without instruments playing. The harmony was pleasing and much louder than in any of the previous events. Many of the children were adding some form of sign language to the mix, probably learned in a Sunday school or midweek program at their church. Brandon could only imagine that God was well pleased with all that was taking place. Whatever hardships or trials the people were facing that week were not written on their faces. The looks were both joyous and peaceful.

The lights came on while the music played. The fire was now glowing embers making the staging area much more visible for everyone. Brandon was pondering what to say, as he waited on the Lord to provide guidance. Then a man tapped him on the shoulder.

> "My name is Avery. I am a school superintendent. One of the high schools in my district is being closed and I was wondering if I could make a donation to your cause here."
>
> "Hi, Avery. My name is Brandon. I don't think we have met before."
>
> "This is my first time here. My son came to an earlier event and invited me."
>
> "Great to have you. What sort of donation do you have in mind?"
>
> "Well, I see the pit filled with various folding chairs and wondered if you would consider something more permanent. The tiered benches around the track and field oval might serve you well, and they need to be removed from the school that is closing anyway. Perhaps, we can help each other."
>
> "Do you think you have enough to fill the pit area?"
>
> "More than enough, and they can be assembled in rows as high as you want."

Brandon thought a moment to visualize rows of tiered benches surrounding the pit. He could see four or, perhaps, five levels high before reaching the yard level. Then he envisioned a few added rows even higher beginning at ground level. The idea added thoughts of better viewing of the stage, additional lighting possibilities and other considerations as well.

"I think you are right. Tiered benches would allow for more people to have seating, better viewing, and less set up work. When are they seats available?"

"The school is already closed so as soon as we can get a crew of men together to help disassemble and haul away, they are yours."

"How can I reach you to coordinate a time?"

"Here's my business card. Just call me anytime. I'm sure we can make it happen quickly."

"I will call you, and thank you for your generous offer."

"You are more than welcome. I think my son will be pleased to know that we can help."

Brandon took the card and placed it in his wallet. David was completing the music program with a word of prayer, inviting the Holy Spirit to come and lead the event. Afterwards, Brandon took the stage and removed the microphone from the stand.

"How's everybody doing?"
A round of boisterous applause followed.

"I guess we can take that as 'great.' It is so wonderful to see so many families here tonight. This is by far our largest crowd. God is in this place. I can feel His presence."

Another round of clapping and "alleluias" followed with many "amen's" intermixed.

"The only agenda that I have is the one I feel led to speak about as God leads me. I have been overwhelmed with the spirit of community expressed by all of you here tonight. I also believe that it is that very spirit that God desires for us."

Then Brandon opened his Bible to the book of Acts and was directed to the verses in chapter 2.

Acts 2:42 – 47 (NIV)

42 They devoted themselves to the apostles' teaching and to the fellowship, to the breaking of bread and to prayer.

43 Everyone was filled with awe, and many wonders and miraculous signs were done by the apostles.

44 All the believers were together and had everything in common.

45 Selling their possessions and goods, they gave to anyone as he had need.

46 Every day they continued to meet together in the temple courts. They broke bread in their homes and ate together with glad and sincere hearts,

47 praising God and enjoying the favor of all the people. And the Lord added to their number daily those who were being saved.

"These are the words God has placed on my heart for you tonight. Now, before we get started, you will not be asked to sell your possessions."

The crowd chuckled.

"You have come here to enjoy a time of fellowship with your family, friends, and even strangers. How many of you have made a new friend tonight?"

The majority raised their hands while many expressed themselves verbally.

"I find that response to be amazing. As I greeted most of you, I was filled with awe. Your children were all smiling, at least the ones I saw. Now, let me ask you another question. How many of you were involved in some way with the donations received on the bus?"

Many hands were raised.

"That just blew me away. Thank you so much for your generosity. No child was left behind tonight as far as having the opportunity to enjoy a smore."

Again there was a roar from the crowd. Even the children chimed in.

"When I felt called to start this ministry, I had no idea where it would lead. Tonight, I am the one who feels led by you. Your community spirit has touched me very deeply. Not only that, but I believe it touches the very heart of God. I do not see anger, worry, doubt, or any other troubling expressions on your faces although I am quite certain that these things are present in your lives. What I see is a genuine desire to want to have a time of joy, fellowship, and peace. It is my prayer that these things will all be yours tonight as we worship the One who gave them to us. I don't know where you stand with your Creator, but I want to let you know that He is real in my life. The love you have demonstrated to one another and to me tonight is just evidence that God is alive."

Once again the crowd erupted with praiseful adoration.

"I don't want to embarrass anyone, but I would like a man to stand for a moment."

Brandon pulled out his wallet to retrieve the business card to read the full name.

"This man approached me tonight with an offer to provide tiered seating around the pit. I look around and see many folding chairs in the pit and on the lawn, but I also can visualize far more people sitting in the same space with elevated benches. Just as I did not solicit the many gifts brought in on the bus, neither did I expect this offer. I would like Mr. Avery Brooks to stand and receive a warm round of applause for his generous offer."

Avery stood up a bit reluctantly and just as quickly sat back down. The applause was well received.

"Mr. Brooks has assured me that the benches are available now, but I will need a crew of able-bodied men to help disassemble and,

somehow, get them over to the farm. Then they need to be assembled again. It sounds like a lot of work, but if God wants us to use them, He will provide a way."

One man yelled out, "I can help." Then another man offered his consent. Before Brandon could speak, more than a dozen fathers offered to help. One man drove trucks for a living and offered a flat bed to haul the benches. He agreed to drop the flatbed off at the school, and then solicit help one evening to take it to the farm. Brandon was speechless. Once again, a large task was reduced to one that was manageable.

"Thank you all for your servant hearts. I guess we need some form of sign-up list so everyone can be contacted."

"No need for that, sir," The man with the truck shouted. *"All I need to know is where to drop off the flatbed. Mr. Brooks can give me that information."*

"Sanford High School," Avery shouted.

"I will drop off the bed near the benches on Sunday. All of you men that would like to help tear down and load, meet me at the school anytime Monday evening after six. If it takes more than one load, I will haul the bed here and return it for another load on Tuesday. If you stop by the school and do not see the bed, then the task was completed."

Just like that, a plan was in place. There was no committee established to review various options and considerations. An opportunity had been provided and hearts were stirred to meet the challenge. Brandon could only wait to see how everything would unfold the following week. Then he addressed the crowd again.

"God has stirred many hearts here tonight to provide needed items for this ministry. I feel so blessed, not only for the donations, but for each of you. Your community spirit is alive, despite the economic and

social woes of these times. I do not see dissension or division among you. Let me ask another question. How many enjoyed the hayride?"

The crowd roared with the children leading the way.

"Now, how many of you enjoyed the fire and a smore or two?"

The response was equally loud.

"Now, how many of you would like this ministry to continue throughout the year?"

This time the decibel levels were even higher as the people stood up. Brandon looked around and saw the faces beaming with excitement as they clapped, hooted, and yelled various support. It took several minutes for everyone to be seated.

"I guess that means that the Wilson farm needs to continue doing what it is doing for a while. Now, I would like to lead you in prayer as my heart goes out to each one of you. I know that we have individual needs, but I would like us to pray silently for one another here tonight. There are two families that have been on my heart all week. Tom and Lucy Wiley are here with us tonight. Would you let the audience know who you are by standing and then sit right back down?"

Tom and Lucy stood, waved, and sat down.

"Is Bob Edwards here?"

There was no response.

"These people have been on my heart because of broken relationships. Bob's teenage daughter left after her mother died and he aches for restoration. Tom's father lost his job several months ago and left without contact as well. Broken relationships are part of what God is all about. He sent His only son, Jesus, to die so that we can have a restored relationship with our Creator. If any of you are going through

similar brokenness, please see me later as I would like to pray for you as well. Tonight, I would ask you to lift up the Edwards and Wiley families with me for healing. Would Tom and Lucy come forward to the stage so that we can lay hands on them? I also encourage anyone else to join us as we pray specifically for this family."

Reluctantly, Tom and Lucy approached the stage. Lucy had tears streaming down her face as Tom placed his arm around her to provide a measure of comfort. Many others joined in a train of hands linked to the Wiley's. Then Brandon, through the leading of the Spirit, led a prayer of reconciliation for them, the Edwards' and for the needs of those families in attendance. Then David closed with a praiseful song.

The Conversion

As the crowds began to leave, Tom and Lucy waited behind until Brandon completed the process of shaking hands and thanking everyone for sharing the evening with him. They watched the process and could not help but feel a strong sense of peace. These were everyday people who had prayed for them. They were warm and outwardly sincere. Then Brandon turned to go back to help douse the fire when he saw them waiting.

"Lucy, why are you still here?"

"I wanted to thank you, personally, for your prayers for us. No one ever did anything like that before. I felt something that I thought I lost."

"What was that, Lucy?"

"Hope. Brandon, I felt hopeful again. I very much desire to see Alan again, but I think a part of me was resolved to the fact that I might not. The prayers of these people gave me hope."

"Jesus is our hope. I never thought I would ever see my father, but here I am living with him again after eighteen years. Do you know Jesus? I mean, do you know Him personally?"

"I am not sure what you mean."

"Have you ever asked Him to be Lord of your life and direct your paths?"

"I believe there is a God and I pray to Him on occasion."

"Do you know why God created us in the first place, Lucy?"

"I guess so that He would have company."

"God doesn't lack for anything. He doesn't need us, but He desires for us to need Him. Of all creation, we are the only life that began from the very breath of God, and we were created in his image."

Brandon went over to the staging area to get his Bible. Then he read the following passages to Tom and Lucy:

Genesis 1:26 – 27 (NIV)
26 Then God said, "Let us make man in our image, in our likeness, and let them rule over the fish of the sea and the birds of the air, over the livestock, over all the earth, and over all the creatures that move along the ground."
27 So God created man in his own image,
in the image of God he created him;
male and female he created them.

Genesis 2:7 (NIV)
7 the LORD God formed the man from the dust of the ground and breathed into his nostrils the breath of life, and the man became a living being.

"Prior creation was spoken into existence, but God took a more personal approach with us. From the beginning, He formed us, breathed life into us, and made us in His own image. In other words, we were set apart for a special purpose. We were given dominion over everything else. We were created in love. I believe that deep down in all of us is a desire to love God in return. You believe in a God, but I want you to know that you can fellowship with Him continuously today. Jesus made the way possible."

"I understand that Jesus came as God's son, showed us how to live by His life, and died, Brandon. But, I don't understand why He did that."

"When creation was over, God said it was 'very good.' But, man was given the gift of free will to choose how to live. God desired that we choose to love Him. He did not want us to react like puppets, but to make conscious choices to love Him in return. Adam and Eve were the first family, and they made a choice to disobey God. That decision allowed sin to enter all mankind. God hates sin. Let me read a couple more passages to you."

Romans 3:23 *(NIV)*
23 for all have sinned and fall short of the glory of God,

Romans 5:8, 12 - 14 *(NIV)*
8 But God demonstrates his own love for us in this: While we were still sinners, Christ died for us.
12 Therefore, just as sin entered the world through one man, and death through sin, and in this way death came to all men, because all sinned 13 for before the law was given, sin was in the world. But sin is not taken into account when there is no law. 14Nevertheless, death reigned from the time of Adam to the time of Moses, even over those who did not sin by breaking a command, as did Adam, who was a pattern of the one to come.

Romans 6:23 *(NIV)*
For the wages of sin is death, but the gift of God is eternal life in Christ Jesus our Lord.

"So, Lucy, Jesus paid the price of sin for us by dying on the cross. As sinners, we deserved the sentence of death. Jesus was without sin. He was blameless, like the lambs offered for atonement in the Old Testament. He did not deserve the punishment of death. He willingly

gave His life for us. God accepted His death as full payment for our sins yesterday, today, and tomorrow."

"So my dept is paid?"

"Yes, but you need to accept it and believe. Let me read one more verse. Perhaps, you have already heard it."

John 3:16 *(NIV)*
16 For God so loved the world that he gave his one and only Son, that whoever believes in him shall not perish but have eternal life.

"Death came into this world because of sin. Until that time Adam and Eve had eternal life and communion with God. We will die earthly deaths, but our souls will reunite with God in heaven. While we are alive on earth, God has sent his spirit to dwell in us as our source of strength, wisdom, and guidance. If the Spirit is within us, then we have fellowship with the Father. Would you like to have joy in you life and a friend in Jesus?"

"I would. What do I need to do?"

"Let God know that you are a sinner, ask for forgiveness, ask Jesus to be Lord of your life, and be baptized. If you truly desire to live a Christ-centered life, then I will help you pray."

"I would like to give my life to Christ. My son has shared many of these things with me in the past. I am ready now."

Tom began weeping uncontrollably. He had been praying for his mother since he accepted Christ as his Savior about a year ago. Brandon led Lucy in prayer, as she became a child of God that evening. The next step was to encourage her to seek a time of baptism. Sundays were workdays at the diner, so she wanted to be baptized at night if possible. Then Tom spoke.

"I would like to be baptized as well. I wonder if we can do it here at the creek. I was so moved by your testimony, Brandon, at the first bonfire."

"You can both be baptized here. The creek is on the chilly side, but if you don't mind, neither do I. It needs to be public, however, so I will ask my church family to come. Is Monday evening around seven okay with you?"

Both Tom and Lucy nodded in agreement.

"I will talk to my pastor and get back to you."
"Thank you, Brandon. Thank you for a wonderful evening," Lucy said as she embraced him.
"I want to warn both of you about something."
"What's that?"
"After I was baptized, many wonderful things started to take place in my life. It was as if God had kept a storehouse of blessings in reserve for me until I completed the act of being baptized. Though my mom passed away, I was reunited with my dad to name a big one. Be prepared for some blessings."

Tom and Lucy made their final embraces and left the farm. There was joy in their steps as they made their way to the car. Brandon thought about his first encounter with Tom and how, shortly afterwards, he was introduced to Lucy at the diner. It was evidence that God was working. The Saturday night hayrides led a new soul into Jesus' open arms.

The next morning came quickly as Brandon could not wait to speak to his pastor about baptism. The events of the evening were so moving that he could not wait to share with the youth group. When the Wiley's arrived at the church, Brandon spotted Tom standing by the front door. Tom waved, excitedly, as he saw Brandon coming towards him.

"Hi, Tom. Long time no see, huh?"
"Mom and I were up until well after midnight just talking. It was wonderful. We have not had conversations like that in a long time and I needed it."

"I think she needed it too, Tom. You lost a father, but it must have been equally hard on her losing a husband."

"Yeah! You're right. She harbored blame and guilt as well. That's what we talked about. It was a time of real healing for both of us and I wanted to thank you again."

"Thank God. He is doing great things in your life. Perhaps, there is a lot more healing to come. A large number of people lifted you both up last night, remember?"

"Before we went to bed, we gave Jesus full rein of whatever would happen in our lives. It was so great to pray like that with mom."

Brandon listened as a tear slowly worked its way down Tom's cheek. The emotion in his voice was further evidence that the time with his mother was special. She spoke about the hope that she felt the night before. Now, the hope was reflected in Tom's Joy.

"Come over and have coffee or juice with me, Tom. I would like to hear more. I will continue to pray that you will get reconciled with your father someday."

"I hope God answers your prayers. That is mine as well."

As the two men were enjoying their drinks, the pastor passed by. Brandon got his attention and motioned for him to join them at the small table.

"Pastor, I need to ask if you would perform a baptism at the farm this week. Monday evening at seven would be good. Tom's mother, Lucy, accepted Christ last night and both of them desire to be dipped in our creek like you did for my mother and me."

"I would be delighted to serve. I have a few things on my calendar tomorrow night, but I can be there at seven. Tom, is it okay with you if I invite the church?"

"You bet, Pastor."

Tom was so excited about all that was happening that he did not hesitate to respond. The time was set. The church family was well represented, and the baptisms took place as scheduled.

THE BENCHES

D uring the baptism, a semi pulled into the field hauling a flatbed filled with benches from the school. Several pickups followed behind as a crew of men began to unload. Brandon could see the trucks from the creek, but their arrival did not disturb the proceedings in any way. As he walked towards the flatbed about half of the bench parts had been unloaded near the pit.

*"Where do you want these?" t*he semi driver shouted. *"We have at least one more load to get. I need to drop the flatbed off at the school tonight for tomorrow's crew."*

"You can stack them on the ground along the three sides of the pit. It looks like you had a pretty good turn out of men to help."

"That we did, Brandon. I think some people came who were not here last night as well."

"How could that be?"

"People talk. They can't wait until next Saturday to come again and they are inviting others."

"If this were a church it would be growing a lot, don't you think?"

"You have a point there. People are searching for something, and they liked what they experienced here. Keep up the good work. We'll get these unloaded and leave quickly. It looks like you have company."

"Tom and Lucy were baptized here tonight. We prayed for them last night, remember?"

"I remember. God sure answers prayer fast."

"They still need our prayers for restoration. Tom's dad is still missing."

"In due time. If it is meant to be, God will bring closure. You can take that to the bank."

"His timing is perfect. We are the ones who are impatient."

"You got it. I will be back tomorrow with the next load."

"Thank you."

Brandon stood at the pit and reflected upon all that had happened in the past week. The crowd on Saturday was much larger than expected; yet everything worked out fine. The additional donated supplies were timely and several boxes were stored for future events. He looked over at the stacks of bench parts and wondered if it were possible to have them installed for the following Saturday's gathering in five days. If not, then they would have to be stored somewhere else to accommodate the crowd. Then he wondered whether the numbers would exceed Saturday's count.

Then a new thought entered Brandon's head. The novelty of something new had brought townspeople back with their neighbors and friends to subsequent events. Unlike a Disney adventure, many of the same people came back. Then he reflected on the activities, which varied. He learned to trust God for each agenda, and without fail, He came through. Could it be the unexpected that allured the people, or something else? God led Brandon to Lucy at the diner, and now her life was changed forever. These and many other thoughts filled his head and heart.

Brandon turned them all over to Jesus in prayer and returned to the house. Jake and Terry were sitting in the living room enjoying a moment of quietness. The children were settled in their rooms for the night.

"Hey, Brandon," Terry said as he entered the room. *"Tonight was very special. Lucy came in to get cleaned up after her baptism and we talked for a while. She is a great lady."*

"Yeah! I must admit that I could not hold back the tears when she went in the water. It was as though my mother was right there as well."

"That creek has special significance to you, Brandon. It always will."

"It's more than that. Mom's gone, but I still feel her presence. God led us to be a family. I mean that it's almost overwhelming. When I was baptized, a dozen or so people were present. Tonight there had to be at least fifty."

"The church supports all that you are doing, Brandon, and welcomes each new member with joy."

"So, when do you want to start assembling the benches?"

"As soon as possible, Dad. It would be great to have them in place for Saturday. Otherwise, we need to move them out of the way to make room for folding chairs."

"I will pick up some bags of cement. We will need to secure the footings."

"I hope the men that disassembled them will know how to put them back together."

"I'm sure we can figure it out. I don't think its rocket science."

Immediately, Brandon's thoughts turned to Lucy and Tom. Rocket science? Tom's dad worked in the space program. Now that Lucy and Tom were baptized, would God bring Alan back to them as he did with his father? There was something about Jake's words that struck a chord in Brandon's heart.

"Dad, would you pray with me right now? I feel led to lift Lucy and Tom up over the return of Alan. Right now, they don't know where he is."

"I would be very pleased to pray with you. If God has placed this burden on your heart right now, then it must be for a reason."

Terry joined them in prayer. Although the time spent was only minutes, it seemed much longer. Brandon could feel the genuine love and concern from his parents as they lifted the family up. At the same time, Brandon's words pierced Jake and Terry's hearts. They prayed together often, especially at the dinner table, but usually for their own family's needs. Tom and Lucy were new converts. There was a sense of urgency as they prayed which felt different somehow. It was as though God was in the room with them and smiling.

"God is going to do something wonderful for this family," Terry said, warmly. *"I don't know what or when, but I sensed His presence tonight"*

"I could feel His arms around us as well," Brandon added.

Jake nodded, as if to say that he felt similar feelings, but his mind turned to other thoughts. He was reminded about turning away from Brandon as a baby. For many of the years that followed, Brandon was a vague memory. When Jake turned his life over to Christ, Brandon's name began to fill his conscious mind. He wondered what Tom's dad was going through at that moment. Was he where he should be with God? Silently, Jake prayed, specifically, for Alan to make peace with his Creator. Instantly, Jake felt a new peace in his life. Brandon was with him as if he had never been apart. For Jake, it was an indescribable feeling, which he kept to himself. It was, however, a milestone in his life. Then he wondered how interceding for someone else could have such a profound impact in his own life.

Jake enjoyed having his son work with him in the plumbing business. Now, he had a strong desire to join him in the ministry on the farm. Up until now, it had been Brandon's calling. Jake helped with construction projects and tending the fire, but a new level of support was placed upon his heart. He did not understand what that would mean, only that he needed to take a higher position of responsibility. Was God calling him like Brandon often shared? The task before them was the erection of the benches, and that was going to be his focus for the week.

"Are there more parts to be delivered, Brandon?"

"Another truckload will be delivered tomorrow night, Dad. I think that will be the last of it."

"Then we will start assembling after work tomorrow. Maybe some of the men unloading can assist in the reconstruction."

"I hope the ones who did the dismantlement will be there. Any tips would help."

"God will provide the instruction if not. He is in the design business." Jake smiled.

"Good thing. I used to have an erector set. The things I built would not hold up well. I think my work would topple if a fly landed on it. The benches need a bit more support don't you think?"

Both men laughed. Terry could sense the male bonding taking place and smiled as well. Then they retired for the night.

Brandon arrived home the next evening around five. His thoughts centered on separating the benches as best he could for their respective positions in the pit. Some parts were still assembled two tiers high, while others were stripped to single benches. As he looked at the task, the term "rocket science" began to take on meaning. He was good at figuring some things out, but this was not one of them. As he moved smaller pieces to the pit area, Jake pulled in. Bags of cement were stacked on the truck bed.

"Got it all figured out?"

"Not exactly. Do you know of any rocket scientists in the area?"

"It can't be that hard. Let's see where we are."

Jake began to look over the barrage of pipes, brackets, and platforms. Some sections still had cement attached.

"These are the foundations. Let's start with them and see where it leads us. Grab an end and we can set them in place."

The front lower tier was obvious. Jake and Brandon had all they could do to lift the first one into the pit. The cement was at least as heavy as the metal parts. Large holes were then dug where the cement fell to allow for new cement to secure them. As the assembly began to take form, the two men began to visualize other parts going together. By the time they had one front row set in place, the second load of parts arrived.

"This is the last of it," The driver shouted. *It looks like you can use some help here."*

"We sure could. These things are heavy. Do we have any mechanical or structural engineers among you?"

A couple men volunteered to lead the assembly effort, while most of the others offered to do the grunt work.

"Great," Brandon responded. *"We can use all the help we can get if we are to have these erected by Saturday."*

"Leave it to me," One volunteer answered. *"You guys just follow my lead and we'll have these up in no time."*

"What's your name, sir?" Jake asked.

"Just call me 'Captain'"

Okay, Captain. Lead on."

The man was slightly built, but began to take charge as if it was second nature to him. The others let him direct. One crew placed sections in the pit while another was ready to fasten them together. Within an hour, one row, three tiers high, took form.

"Leave those bolts a little loose, guys. Don't snug them up yet. Once the entire frame is assembled, we can make the final tightening."

There was something in Captain's voice that indicated that he knew what he was doing. The process continued for two more hours with the pit nearly full. The three sides were now six tiers high with the last one assembled on the lawn height. The men agreed to take a break for the evening as they were now working under the lights. The shadows made visibility difficult. Most of the remaining pieces were placed where they could be assembled so a smaller crew could finish the work. Captain's presence was essential to complete the task, however. It was one thing to see the benches erected and in place, but quite another to know they would safely support a crowd of people.

"I can come down during the day, tomorrow if that is okay with you, Jake?"

"I will leave the gate open. Come anytime, Captain. I can join you if you like."

"That would be great. I would love to have someone to talk to as I work. It is so much better to work with someone."

"Done then. I will finish up some things in the morning at work and come home by noon. How 'bout joining me for lunch here, say 12:30?"

"12:30 it is. I will see you then."

"Brandon, that means that you will have to take up the slack at work." Jake added with a smirk knowing that Brandon had things well under control.

"I do your work anyway," Brandon quickly snapped back.

"You guys have a great relationship," the Captain shared in observation. *"I have a son, but I never had that kind of relationship."*

"Thank you, Captain. We're catching up on a lot of lost time. We'll pray for you and your son to have a great relationship."

The Captain nodded as if to say thanks and headed to an old beat up small truck. The paint was almost unrecognizable, and several parts were missing. Jake noticed it and made a comment.

"For a captain, you seemed to have gotten the short straw in the motor pool."

"It may have a lot of miles, Jake, but it gets me around."

"That's all that matters then. See you tomorrow."

"You bet. I look forward to it."

TIE DOWNS

J ake and Brandon looked back at the assembly and marveled. The tiers of seating were not fully secured, but they could visualize people filling them on Saturday. There was something wholesome and assuring about the Captain. He knew exactly what he was doing.

"It looks like there are enough parts still to be assembled that we may have nine or ten levels before all is done, Dad."

"By the way, I called the town to see if we needed a permit. The answer is that we do, but it should be approved without any problems. I will stop by the town hall and fill it out."

"I never thought about that, Dad. Thanks. It would be a shame to assemble everything only to have to tear it down later."

"We cannot let people use the seating until a structural engineer inspects it and gives his or her approval."

"Do you know of anyone, or does the town supply somebody?"

"The board will provide a list of names for me to call. I guess these people have their credentials registered so they can be called on. There may be a fee associated, but I will take care of that."

"No, Dad. We will take care of that. We are a team. I think God wants this ministry to be OUR ministry."

"I think you are right, but we are just His tools. It is God's ministry."

The next day, Jake left the worksite early and headed for the courthouse to file the permit. A list of inspector names was handed to him with phone numbers. The construction could continue, but usage was dependent on passing the inspection. Once the seal-of-approval was attached to the permit, the benches could be used. That process sounded urgent if they were to conduct a gathering on Saturday. Nevertheless, Jake was certain that God was in total control. He led them this far, and would make a way, like the Israelites at the Red Sea.

When Jake arrived home, the Captain's truck was in the yard. Lunch was nearly ready.

"Good afternoon, Captain."

"Hello, Jake. Your wife has a big pot of homemade soup. The aroma when I came in was wonderful. I have not had good home-cooked food in quite a while"

"That's why I married her," Jake said as he affectionately embraced Terry,

"I can understand that, but why on earth did she accept your proposal?"

There was something in the Captain's voice that struck a chord with Jake. His attempt at humor brought a smile from Terry. Jake smiled as well, but there was a wee small voice in his head that desired to get to know the man better. The Captain's face held a small grin, but it appeared superficial. Jake wondered why he had the feelings that he did and silently asked God for discernment. After the soup was placed into bowls on the table, everyone sat down. Jake led them in prayer.

"Lord, we thank You for this food and for our new friend who is able to share it with us today. Bless this food to our nourishment and the hands that prepared it. Bless our time today at the pit. May we

be kept safe and Your work be completed. Bless Captain and all that is going on in his life. May his goals and dreams be realities. In the precious name of Jesus, Amen."

Jake looked up and saw a tear beginning to fall by the Captain's eye.

"What's wrong, Captain?"

"I guess I was moved by your prayer, Jake. No one has ever prayed a blessing like that for me before, at least none that I have heard."

"Don't you pray?"

"Not as I should. When I can't fix something, I scream more than pray."

"God can fix anything. Do you believe that?"

"I believe that this world was not a series of accidents like the school textbooks seem to lead us to believe. There must have been a creator or a host of them."

"You sound as though a creator came and is no longer with us. Do you actually believe that?"

"I don't know what to believe. My father told me that my life's worth is measured by how well I provide for my family. I had everything going for me, namely, a six-figure income, great family, nice home, and new vehicles. My dad would have been proud if he were still alive."

"How long has be been gone?"

"Nearly two years now. Not long afterwards, I lost my job. They said it was due to attrition, but I think my work suffered after his loss."

"What did you do for a living?"

"I was an aerospace structural engineer. I worked for NASA at the Cape."

Jake's jaw dropped. Could this be Tom's father? If so, then things were beginning to make sense. The benches had been delivered and shortly afterwards, this man appeared with all the right skills to make it happen. Then Jake thought about the paper he received from the town board with the names of structural engineers. He excused himself and went to his truck to retrieve the list. He returned a few moments later. One name caught his eye.

"Tell me Captain, are you Alan Wiley?

"I am. Now I am curious as to how you know me."

"First, your name is on the list of structural engineers that I was given today. We will need one to approve the work when it has been completed."

"There must be dozens of names on that list. Why did you associate that name with me."

"Do you have a son named, Tom and a wife named, Lucy?"

Alan looked down at the floor and began weeping. Hearing the names of his family opened an emotional outlet.

"I still don't understand, Jake. How do you know my family?"

"Tom came to our first bonfire. My son, Brandon, gave his testimony that night about how I came back into his life. I had been a foolish young father, caught up in about everything bad. Drugs, alcohol, and a life of crime were all part of my past. Brandon never knew me until this past year. Later, Tom came forward and shared his story about losing a dad and how he longed for reconciliation. He felt guilty, as if he caused his father to leave."

"But he didn't. I tried to get work to support my family. I felt that it was better for me to break away. I was afraid my frustration would turn to anger and I might do something I would regret and harm them."

"Your leaving harmed them. Your father instilled the wrong values in you. Life is not about how many things we accumulate. Houses, cars, and all of those so-called luxuries are not taken with us when we die."

"I wanted to come home, but I felt that I disgraced them. I got a room at one of the schools and supported myself as a maintenance mechanic. The superintendent called me to help with these benches."

"It's strange that the very night the first load was dropped off, Lucy and Tom were being baptized in the creek at the back of the property."

"Lucy and Tom were here?"

"They were probably in the house getting cleaned up when you arrived."

The news seemed to set off a host of emotions as Alan glared at Jake. He thought that it was strange that the superintendent asked him to help reassemble the benches on private property. The hours spent were even added to his paycheck. The idea that his wife and son were all part of the picture made him consider that his life was under a microscope. The things that were happening could not possibly be coincidences. The past year was one of total isolation for Alan. Puzzle books and brainteaser problems consumed his evenings, except for short trips for groceries. The old truck served to haul items for the school more than transportation. Suddenly, a floodgate had opened, and Alan needed to take action.

"Don't you want to see your family, Alan? If for no other reason, you need to let your son know that he is not to blame for your leaving.. I think Lucy harbors guilt as well."

"I need time to think about what I would say. This has been a real shock."

"Do you want peace in your life, Alan?"

"I wrestle with a lot of things. I think I have a lot of demons inside me."

"The peace I desire for you will rid those demons and bring joy. Would you like to know how to find that joy?"

"I thought I had joy in my life, until my dad died. Losing my job plunged me into a pit of utter despair. I would love to find those feelings of joy that I have lost. I sense that you are a true friend, Jake. I need a friend like you."

"I am your friend, Alan, but I want you to have a friend who is even better than I. You try to solve everything with your head. Putting the pieces together like a jigsaw puzzle is impossible when you don't have all the pieces. God sees the big picture. He led you here. You are not here by chance. Do you believe that?"

"Things could not have happened like this by accident. Someone or something must be pulling the strings."

"You said that you believe we were created. Doesn't it make sense that our Creator would leave a manual to help us to make needed repairs?"

"I guess, especially, if the Creator would leave to make new things elsewhere."

"The manual is right here. It's called, the Bible. It teaches us many things about our physical and flawed body. The best part is that it lets us know that the Creator never left. It talks about a love that surpasses anything we can imagine. Do you want to know how to mend your broken heart? I would love to show you and help you find true peace in your life."

"I would, Jake. I truly would."

Jake took Alan into the living room where he began to read scripture. After each reading, he asked Alan if he understood what the words meant. Alan began to see how everything fit together and the puzzle began to take shape. Scales of bitterness, resentment, guilt, and shame slowly lost their weight. Alan accepted Jesus as his Savior and desired to receive the same baptism as his wife and son at the creek. Jake assured him that it would take place.

"How wonderful would it be if your wife and son were here to witness the event, Alan?"

"I would like that."

"Lucy works at the diner on weekends. Would you like to go with me on Saturday to see her?"

"I need some time to digest things. I will let you know."

"Did you know that last Saturday we prayed for you as a family here? Dozens of people came down and placed their hands on Tom and Lucy at the pit. We prayed for your reconciliation. How does that make you feel now?"

"God answers prayer very quickly."

"Sometimes, the answers are quick. I accepted Jesus some eight years before Brandon came into my life. We don't know God's timing, but we can be assured that it is never late. Let's see what we can do with the benches. You can make a decision later about meeting Lucy. I can tell you, however, that she loves and misses you more than you can possible know."

"I just need a little more time. Let's get these benches completed while we have daylight."

"You got it, Alan, or should I call you Captain?"

"Call me friend," Alan responded with a smile that could light up a room.

Jake returned an equally large smile. Alan headed towards the front door while Jake went to locate a spare Bible.

"Just a minute, Alan. I want you to have something. Take this Bible and find some quiet time to read. It will help you make the decisions that you need to make."

"Thank you, Jake. I will."

The rest of the afternoon was spent on securing the benches. Alan provided the leadership while Jake followed the instructions. Cement footings were poured to secure the existing tiers at the lower level. In addition, steel wires were anchored for secondary support. Special care was taken to ensure that the construction would sustain high winds and people. All of the fittings were tightened once the alignment was completed. The remaining benches were set loosely in place at the ground level above the pit. The rows facing the stage area would be ten high when completed while the other two sides reached nine levels. At least two hundred people could sit comfortably.

As the two men were working, Brandon arrived. He parked near the barn and could see the two men busily making final preparations. They were laughing and acting as though they had been friends for a long time. The scene seemed strange, but refreshing at the same time. He started walking down the path to the pit when Jake shouted:

> *"Hey, Brandon. I want you to meet someone."*
> *"I already met the Captain, remember."*
> *"Yeah, but there's someone else that you need to meet."*

Brandon looked around to locate another person. Only Jake and the Captain were to be seen as he approached the pit. The rows of seats sparkled in the bright sunlight.

> *"Okay, where's this other person? I only see you guys here."*
> *"The Captain is a new person. He accepted Jesus today."*
> *"That is wonderful. Heaven must be rejoicing as well. The benches look terrific. How soon can they be used?"*
> *"The cement will be settled this time tomorrow. We hope to have everything in place by Friday, including the final inspection."*
> *"God is moving quickly,"* Brandon responded.

Jake was about to introduce the Captain as Alan Wiley, but Alan cleared his throat as if to say that the time was not right.

RECONCILIATION

J ake honored Alan's wishes to keep his identity in confidence. Alan discussed a few other options for the pit, including additional lighting, rain protection, and lightning rods, which Jake could discuss later with Brandon. Alan had a wealth of knowledge and seemed genuinely enthused about being involved in the project. Brandon joined Jake in prayer for Alan's family decisions as the three men gathered together. After Alan left, Jake advised Brandon to not say anything to Tom or Lucy until Alan gave the okay.

When Jake returned to the house, Terry could sense an extra spring in his step and a glow on his face.

"So, Honey, what are you so happy about? You must have had a good day at work."

"I don't know about that. Brandon carried the load, unless you are referring to the benches. They sure came out great"

"There is something going on with you, Jake Wilson. I haven't seen you like this since the day you were baptized."

"Alan accepted Jesus tonight. Heaven has a new guest."

"That's wonderful. You'll have to tell me the whole story now."

Jake led Terry into the living room and began to share. He reflected on all that had happened that night as well as his call to serve with Brandon in the pit ministry. He shared about Alan's life, but reminded Terry that she was not to say anything outside the home unless Alan gave the approval.

"God is doing great things right here. You and Brandon have been called to serve."

"Yeah, and He is working out every detail. I think the excitement that you read on my face comes from my anticipation for what He will do next. The pieces are coming together at lightning speed."

"I'll say. Even though you abandoned your son as an immature father, God had foundations in place for reconciliation. Now, He is using both of you for a greater purpose."

"Amazing, isn't it?"

"Now, we need to see how the restoration between Alan and his family takes shape. Do you know when Alan will be baptized?"

"I will call the pastor tomorrow. I know that Saturday night before the bonfire would be good since Alan will be there."

"Wouldn't it be wonderful if Lucy and Tom witnessed it?"

"That is exactly what I shared with Alan, Honey. I hope he contacts them between now and Saturday."

Jake and Terry had learned to wait on God. They knew that He was never late. His timing was always perfect. Still, the anticipation of how God would work left both of them feeling a bit anxious. They knew that the Wiley family had been entrusted to them for a purpose. Before they retired for the night, Brandon joined them.

"I'm so proud of you, Dad. It feels pretty good to help someone find their way home, doesn't it?"

"You bet. If I had stayed at work and let you work with Alan, then you would have done the same."

"That may be so, but God wanted you to be there. I think He wants this ministry to be a joint effort."

"I will serve any way that I can. You know that."

"I know you support me, Dad. This venture has been planned before I was born. Your experiences will play a role. You went through a lot, and God intends to use it for good. Count on it."

"We can be a team, Son, but don't ask me to lead. I am better one-on-one."

"If God wants you to lead, you will have the skills. I enjoy being with people, but I don't consider myself a leader."

"You could have fooled me."

"Thanks, Dad, but my strength comes from the Lord. Yours will too."

Friday came and the town's approval for the bench use was official. Alan had taken care of the details. Jake made arrangements with the pastor to assist in the baptism at the start of the festivities on Saturday. Tom and Lucy had yet to be contacted, as Alan still felt a bit uneasy. Jake agreed to help out since Alan expressed his desire to have them there at the baptism. Jake went to the diner the following morning while Alan waited outside for his cue to come in.

"Good morning, Lucy. How's your breakfast here? My son raves about it."

"We have eggs any way you like them, old fashioned home fries with bacon, ham, or sausage specials until nine."

"Great! I'd like my eggs over medium with sausage and rye toast."

"You got it. Can I add coffee?" You can. Cream and sugar would be great/."

"Coming right up. Tom and I are looking forward to this evening as well. I'll be right back with your coffee."

Jake watched her leave and thought about how he could introduce the subject of Alan's return and desire for reconciliation. Silently, he prayed for wisdom. Alan could see Jake from outside the diner and nervously awaited Jake's hand gesture, which was the signal to enter. Lucy returned quickly with the coffee.

"Thank you, Lucy. I wanted to ask you about your husband. Do you mind? I know Tom misses him very much."

"As do I. I miss him terribly."

"I think Tom holds some guilt over his leaving. How do you feel about it?"

"Losing his father and then his job took a heavy toll on Alan. I may not have been the most supportive wife, although I tried."

"So, Lucy, if Alan came back today, how would that make you feel?"

"Elated. I pray every day for his return."

With those words, Jake made the agreed hand gesture and Alan entered. Jake could hear the door open, but Lucy had her eyes on Jake. The discussion had caught her curiosity, and she wondered why Jake brought up the subject. She knew her family had been lifted up by the ministry at the pit, but this was the first time Jake came into the diner while she was working.

"Lucy, you know we have been praying for you and your family."

"Yes, and Tom and I really appreciate it a lot."

"Our prayers have been answered this week. God sent Alan to us and I think he wants to say a few words to you."

"I am always open to hear from God."

"No, I mean Alan wants to share."

With those words, Jake motioned towards the door, causing Lucy to turn around. Alan's eyes pierced her heart and tears of joy flowed. She could not contain herself and ran towards her husband with arms open wide. Alan stopped as if to brace himself.

"Lucy, my darling Lucy. I've missed you so much."

Jake sat back and watched. If no words were spoken, volumes were still felt. Patrons began to clap as if the meeting was part of a successful play and they made up the audience. God had performed another miracle. Shortly afterwards, a new waitress noticed that Lucy was preoccupied and brought out Jake's breakfast.

"Lucy, take a break. I'll cover for you," she offered.

"Thanks, Joanne. Can you bring a couple of cups of coffee over for my husband and me?"

"You bet. Let me know if he wants something to eat with that."

"Just coffee", Alan said as the tears continued to roll down his cheeks.

Jake looked at Alan as if to see if he desired support. He would welcome them to sit with him, but also knew that they needed to be alone. Alan sensed Jake's intent and told him that they would get a table in the back of the diner. Words were not spoken. Jake simply nodded and they left. The experience warmed Jake's heart. The baptism that evening would be a fitting climax as Tom would be there as well.

Jake motioned to the new waitress to bring his check, and she let him know that the bill had been paid. Her words brought thoughts of Jesus paying the price for Jake's sins on the cross almost as if that had been the intent. As Jake was about to leave the diner, he caught Lucy's eye and nodded as a way of saying thank you for the breakfast. The joy of reconciliation was written all over her face as she waved back.

Jake returned home and discussed all that had happened with Terry. They paused to offer their humble thanks to God for the miracle in the Wiley family and asked for continued guidance in the activities for that evening. Two families were uplifted on the very first bonfire meeting. Now, they witnessed answered prayers for one of them. Their thoughts turned to the Edwards' family, and they prayed for peace in that family as well. As far as they knew, Bob still had not heard from his daughter after she blamed him for her mother's suicide.

Brandon left that morning to complete a plumbing job. He knew that his father planned on talking to Lucy at the diner and anxiously came home to find out what had happened.

"So, Dad, how did it go at the diner this morning?"

"Great, Brandon. When I left, Lucy and Alan were having a conversation alone. I could hear some laughter as well."

"Do you think the whole family will be here tonight?"

"I do, Son."

"I am so excited for them."

"I can't wait for this evening. The Holy Spirit is moving already."

THE BAPTISM

The cars and buses began to arrive shortly after five. Many came expecting to help set up chairs and prepare tables for various food items. The preassembled benches pleasantly surprised them. The pastor had made the announcement of Alan's baptism through electronic mail and phone calls so many arrived early for that event.

Jake was preparing the kindling and firewood at the pit, but kept looking up towards the visitors. His thoughts were on Alan, Lucy and Tom. He wondered if they would come as a family. Would they have joy in their steps? Would they all attend the baptism? The joy of leading Alan to Jesus was still fresh on Jake's heart as he pondered these questions. With each passing minute, the expectations continued to elevate his anxiousness.

The pastor arrived about fifteen minutes before the scheduled baptism time and spotted Jake at the pit.

"Great day in the Lord, isn't it, Jake?"

"You bet, Pastor. I think it will be an even greater evening."

"You may be right there, Jake. I did my best to alert the congregation so that they can be here to support Alan."

"I think many are already here. Some have asked where the baptism will take place as this is the first time they've been here."

"Then they are in for a treat as well."

"Thank you for the compliment. I don't know what has been planned. Brandon handles that part of the festivities, and he usually fires from the hip as God leads."

"You cannot go wrong there. God does amazing things."

"That He does. I think I see Alan coming."

Alan, Tom, and Lucy arrived together and were walking along the path near the barn towards the pit. Jake could not see their facial expressions, but he sensed joy in their walk. Lucy walked along side Alan holding his hand. Tom was close behind looking around as if he were searching for someone in particular. The scene held Jake captive for a moment. A family had been reunited. Suddenly, Tom took off towards the house.

"Brandon, Brandon, my dad's come home."

The yelling was so loud that Jake heard it over the crowd noise several hundred feet away. The exuberance in Tom's voice was unmistakable. The joy in his heart over the return of his father could not be restrained. Tonight it would be even amplified by Alan's baptism. Prior to his leaving, God was only a buzzword. Tonight, they are a new family with God as the head.

"Welcome, Tom. You have got to show some joy," Brandon said with a snicker.

"Last night was totally awesome. For the first time we sat down together and talked. I mean, really talked."

"I am so happy for you. Since my dad returned to my life, we talk all the time."

"For the first time in my life, I feel like we are a family. Dad's work kept us apart in the past. Now, it's like he is a new man. Work is far less important."

"Perhaps your father needed to learn that lesson."

"I have no doubt of that. I am excited to be here and observe his baptism."

"I am as well, Tom."

Brandon and Tom headed towards the baptism site, where Lucy and Alan were going over the details with the pastor. A few clouds dotted the sky, but no rain was in the forecast. The water was warm and perfect for the ceremony. As Tom approached, he noticed his mother's arm gently rubbing his father's neck. Alan was returning the gesture. The scene left Tom with a warm feeling about his parents. The pain and guilt that he had felt during his father's absence was slowly melting away. The pool of water held a common bond for the Wiley family. The future seemed so much brighter.

The baptism was only a few minutes away. Alan came prepared with a change of clothes in the car. Brandon made his way towards the stage area and turned on a microphone. After testing the sound, he made the announcement for the crowd to gather at the cross. The fallen tree was still held up forming the shape. The people gathered close together to witness the event. The creek was several feet below ground level, making the gentle slope down from the property somewhat like a small amphitheater. It were as if God had prepared that detail in advance as well. Between seventy-five and a hundred people were in attendance. A rope was hung over the pool to secure a wireless mike for the crowd to hear.

The pastor slowly made his way into the water as Alan followed. They positioned themselves below the mike. The water was nearly four feet deep and clear. The rainy season would stir up the bottom making the water muddy in appearance. The crowd could see Alan's feet nestled in the soil on the bottom. As Lucy and Tom stood in front of the tree-made cross, it cast a shadow on Alan.

"Look at that, Mom. Dad is totally covered by the shadow of a cross."

"I noticed that as well, Son. Perhaps, God is trying to tell us something."

"Yeah! I think He wants us to know that all is well in the Wiley family today."

"I think He wants us to remember this moment. We may go through more hard times, but today, we can be certain that we will not go through those times alone again."

The pastor opened with prayer and then asked Alan if he had received Jesus Christ as his personal Savior. Alan quickly responded, *"Yes."* A tear began to fall down Lucy's cheek. Her commitment was still fresh on her heart and mind. For much of their lives they relied on themselves to meet the challenges of each day. Now they had a resource in Jesus that went beyond human logic. Lucy had been reunited with her husband less than a day, but she could feel a real sense of peace. Alan was then baptized. As he came out of the water, a cloud blocked the sun. The shadow of the cross was no longer visible.

"The shadow is gone, Mom. What do you think it means?"

"I think that God has cast a blanket on all of us. I don't think it was a coincidence."

"Neither do I. I think God is blanketing us with His love."

"Now that's comforting, Tommy."

Lucy smiled at her son, as she knew that name would bring out a response. Tom understood and returned the gesture. As Alan came up onto the bank, he could see the smiles on their faces and his heart leaped with joy. The life he had known was no longer the one he would live. God and family came before work. The words of his father seemed to flow away like the current in the creek. He desired to live his life to please his Lord and Savior. Somehow, being a janitor and having a wife who waited on tables was okay. If the future held a different path for Alan, then God would direct him. Lucy held a towel in her outstretched arms and embraced Alan with it as he approached.

"I just want you to know how proud I am of you. I love you, Alan Wiley."

"I love you, too. I always have. For the first time in my life I feel real peace."

"I feel that peace as well, Honey. This past year has been tough. Tonight, I feel the scales of worry, guilt, and doubt fall."

"Guilt? I left, not you."

"I could have been more supportive of your work. I felt that I was one of the reasons why you left."

"It was never about you except for my feelings of inadequacy to support you and Tom. Please, forgive me for causing you to feel that way."

"Of course I forgive you. I love you. I have always loved you. Now we can be the family that God wants us to be."

"Lucy, have you ever considered that everything has happened for a reason...my work, my dad's passing, I mean all of it leading us to this point? I think God has more for me to do, and I desire to serve Him."

"All I know is that I have never been happier than I am right now, and that is because of Jesus. Whatever He wants you to do, I am sure that we will be doing it together."

Tom pulled the towel aside and hugged his father. One by one, the guests came up to them to offer their congratulations. The Wiley family was deeply touched by the warmth of the heartfelt welcome into the family of God. The act of baptism was Alan's open desire to let the world know that he was a child of God. The affirmation of the witnesses offered an extra measure of comfort. Many of them desired to see the Wiley family in church, which Alan felt led to do as well. There was a lot more to learn about following Christ. Lucy's work at the diner had limited any Sunday morning church services, but if God had led them this far, then surely, He would lead them further.

As the three of them moved towards the house to get cleaned up, Brandon announced that the hayrides were about to begin. Ol' Betsy was fired up, and the sound caused the children to run to the wagon. The activities of the evening were officially started. The seating around the pit was populated with various bags, water bottles and other placeholders as people began to mark their desired seats. Jake had the logs and kindling ready to accept a match. The band began to set up their instruments and test the sound system.

The activities for the evening were still up in the air. Brandon wanted to introduce Alan and his family as new entries into God's kingdom as well as answers to the prayers offered by the attendees since the first bonfire. The prayers to reunite the Wiley family were wonderfully answered. Not only were they a family again, but also now they were part of an eternal family. Brandon planned on asking Alan to speak, if he desired. As in the past events, Brandon trusted God to provide any additional message.

THE TESTIMONY

W hile families enjoyed their turn on the hayride, others were getting to know Tom, Lucy, and Alan. Jake and Brandon observed the interaction.

"So, Brandon, isn't it wonderful to see a family reunited?"

"Yeah, especially in Christ. That swimming hole has blessed several people. I want to ask you something, Dad."

"Ask away."

"When you were baptized, did you feel anything special?"

"Like what?"

"I mean, different than before. I think God adds some extra measure of blessings when we take that step and acknowledge our commitment in that way."

"I know that my life changed, Son. I am not sure if there were fireworks or anything like that."

"As I watch the Wiley family, I see blessings all around them. They are united again. The family of God surrounds them."

"My plumbing business took off shortly after my baptism. Come to think of it, that's when I met your uncle. I guess I received more blessings, too."

"I lost mom shortly after my ceremony, but then you came into my life, Dad."

"I bet you never thought that this farm would be used as a gathering place for people like it is now either."

"It might be a good question to ask Jesus when we come into His presence, don't you think?"

"I think that He supplies everything we need and then some after we take a public stand for Him. Maybe the blessings are His way of saying, 'well done.'"

"Maybe. It's still great to see the Wiley's so happy. I asked Alan to say a few words at the fire tonight and he accepted."

"I can't wait to hear him speak. You are doing such a wonderful job leading these proceedings."

"God's doing the leading, Dad. I am just His servant."

The wagon rides provided enjoyable family time for everyone. Happy faces disembarked and headed to the snack tables where zip-locked bags of marshmallows awaited. Mom or dad carefully selected the metal tipped cooking rods and headed to the stands. By the time the hayrides were half through, Jake had the fire well under control. The ashes were ready to accept the marshmallows, and the children were more than eager to roast them. Jake had learned the art of fire preparation. The raging fires of his childhood were now carefully orchestrated beds of coal on a ten-foot square pit. The heat was bearable from a few feet away.

As the sun began to fall, the coals took on brilliant orange, red, and yellow colors. It were as if the auburn sunset were being captured in their glow. Shortly after the sun left the horizon, the band began to play. That was the sign for families to assist their children in putting away their rods and taking their seats. Within a few minutes the floodlights came on and the stage was illuminated. David opened the worship time with prayer and then led the group in familiar praise songs. Many of the children began to apply some form of dance or signing to the words, which caught Brandon's eye. Although he had not had been taught these things as a child, he witnessed them in various events involving the children at the church. It was obvious to him that hayrides and music had a big effect on everyone, especially the children.

When the music stopped, David motioned for everyone to take his or her seat. Then he introduced Brandon to offer the message. Silently, Brandon prayed for the Holy Spirit to lead him as he walked up the steps. He then gave David a warm embrace and thanked him for his leadership. David placed the microphone in Brandon's hand and proceeded to join the audience.

"This has been a terrific night already.

The audience agreed with a thunderous roar.

"How do you like the new benches?"

Again the shouts of appreciation rang out from the crowd.

"Many people helped make this addition a reality this week. When the offer of the benches first came, I must admit that I thought any implementation would be a long time away, but willing hearts, minds, and muscles joined in to make the reality happen in one week. I would like to ask all of the people who helped this week to stand so we can give them our appreciation."

Alan stood, along with at least a dozen others. The people clapped and cheered. Some stomped their feet on the benches as if to say, "well done." Nearly two hundred people were in attendance. The enthusiasm could be seen on each face. The numbers increased every week as evidence that the event was special to each family. Friends invited other friends. Brandon could see many new faces in the crowd.

"Many of you arrived early tonight to witness a baptism. During our very first bonfire, we prayed for the Wiley family. Tonight, you witnessed answered prayer as only God can do. Not only has the

Wiley family been reunited, but also each of them has surrendered to Christ as their Savior and Lord. God is so great."

Once again the crowd erupted in praise. They stood to acknowledge the Wiley family. More importantly, they recognized God's amazing grace and power. Alan, Lucy and Tom waved back in acknowledgement. There was a special joy in the air as the people could not seem to contain themselves. After several minutes, Brandon was able to continue.

"I asked Alan if he would say a few words to us tonight. As you know, this time is about sharing together, especially, what God has done in our lives. We go through life believing at times that our trials are unique. Perhaps, some of you are going through similar things, like the Wiley family. Their story may inspire you. Please welcome Alan as he shares his story with us."

As Alan made his way up to the stage, the crowd stood and gave a joyous welcome. Lucy and Tom sensed the acceptance as they joined in as well. Brandon could see Alan's face light up as he walked closer. The life of isolation, which Alan had had in the small room in the school basement, was now a memory.

"Thank you, Brandon. Thank you for everything."
"I didn't do anything, Alan. God had your back all along."
"That He did. I just didn't see it before."
"Please, speak to us from your heart." With that, Brandon passed the mike to his friend.

"Good evening. I am not known for my speaking ability so please bear with me. It is my prayer that the Lord guides my words to you."

A moment of cheering provided a pause for Alan to gather himself.

"Like many of you, I had a dream as a young man to be successful, raise a family, and the other facets of the American dream. My father instilled many things in me, just as your parents may have in you. He

told me that a man was measured by how well he provided for his family. Dad was a work-a-holic. When he was at home, I learned how to do things with my hands, but I cannot remember very many times when we shared things together outside of the work environment. For me, being a dad meant providing for my children's comfort needs. Being a husband meant paying the bills. I truly believed that everything my father told me was gospel."

Alan paused and scanned the crowd. He could sense that many of them had been taught similar lessons. Some murmuring could be heard, but there was a sense of great anticipation in their faces. Alan's words had set the stage for hearts to receive a testimony. Alan, silently, prayed for wisdom before he continued.

"My father passed away nearly two years ago. I felt a huge loss. There was a void inside of me that needed filling, and I could not find anything suitable to fill the emptiness that I held inside. It affected my work, my family, and everything else in my life. My dad was my source of strength and now that source was lost. I'm sure that many of you can relate."

Once again, Alan paused. He could see heads nodding.

"I am here tonight to let you know that we are not measured by how many toys we have. My dad was wrong. I can't believe I am saying that. Only a few months ago, I would have defended my father with my life. I still love him. I still miss him terribly, but I have learned that life is not about providing things. Rather, it is much more about receiving. God wants to give us every good gift. He stands at our heart's door and knocks. He was knocking at my door, but I refused to answer for far too long. Please, I implore you to answer His call. We do not know the time or date when we will leave this earth so now is the time if you haven't received Jesus Christ in your life. I didn't know

that the void in my life needed to be filled with the love of my Savior until meeting Jake and Brandon here at the pit."

Jake stood up and made his way to the stage. He could sense Alan's call to join him. Alan's words brought sighs and cheers in the crowd as Jake walked up the stairs. As he approached, Alan stepped away from the mike and met Jake with a warm embrace. Words did not need to be spoken, but volumes were heard in the exchange.

"Alan, my friend, God has had His eye on you all along. Your father may be gone, but your Heavenly Father will never leave you."

"I know that now, thanks to you, Jake."

"Don't thank me. Thank God. I am just a servant like you are tonight. Your story needs to be shared wherever you go. I am certain that there are many people going through the same types of events and can use your testimony. Please continue."

"I am sharing here tonight as a changed man. The love I have for my family has been magnified by the added love that I now have from my Savior, Jesus Christ. My son will have a father, who provides many things, but none of them will be more important than this message, namely, Jesus loves you. He is bigger than the entire universe, yet He loves one small speck named, Alan Wiley. My technical background makes that incomprehensible. Yet, I know He loves me. I know that He loves my wife, my son, and everyone of you here tonight. He desires to come into every heart and fellowship. I am so thankful that when I reach the limits of my strength and knowledge, God's resources are still available for the asking.

The crowd erupted with joyous affirmation. As they shouted 'alleluia' and 'amen,' the lights came on with a soft glow. By the time the crowd sat down, the lights were at full intensity. It was almost eerie. What was about to be said seemed to take on an even higher significance by the effect. To Alan, the glow placed a shadow on the audience. Faces appeared less discernable. For a moment it took him by surprise, yet he felt great peace. Then he continued.

"When I lost my job at the space agency, I thought my whole world collapsed. First, my dad passed away, and then my job ended. I felt helpless and hopeless after long searches on the web for new employment. The economic climate placed huge limitations on finding work that would come anywhere close to the standards I was used to. I traveled outside the city and the state to find relief. When I came back, I could not face my family. I felt that I had let them down. I took a job at the school and an old couch became my bed in the basement. I wondered, how much lower could I sink. Have any of you ever felt that way?"

Alan could see many faces nodding.

"Is Avery here tonight? My superintendent, Avery Brooks, if you are here, please yell out."

"I'm here, Alan." Avery stood for a moment and sat back down.

"Avery, I want you to know that you were God's servant. When I was at my lowest moment, you stepped in. You gave me some purpose in life, even if it meant repairing broken desks or tearing down benches. I never dreamed that the work would lead me here, but God had it all under control. Thank you, Avery, for responding to God's call as you did."

Avery nodded and the crowd affirmed Alan's words with an applause.

I have just a few more things to say, as I feel led. Please bear with me. I know that someone listening tonight needs God's grace, mercy, and unending love and silently I am praying for you. My life as an aerospace structural engineer was no accident. The benches you are sitting on came from a school, which had closed due to the economy. It was no coincidence that I was working there when someone was needed to help dismantle them and erect them here. The town's ordinance required a structural engineer's signature to complete the task, and my name was on the list. Last week, those seats were at the school. Tonight they have the town's seal of approval and you are enjoying the view."

Again, the audience cheered.

"God sees the much bigger picture. We get so caught up in the walls around us that we cannot see the forest outside. I cannot wait to see where God leads my family and me in the future. But, I know that it will be far better than anything I can plan or think. I still do not have a high paying job, but for the first time in my life, I have real peace. I would like my wife and son to join me here now. I don't want to embarrass them, but I want you to know them. Outside of my Savior, they are everything to me."

Lucy and Tom stood and made their way to the platform. Tom looked anxious to greet his dad, but held back some enthusiasm to stay in pace with his mother. Slowly, they climbed the steps as Alan walked towards them. He held out his arms and they warmly embraced. After a moment, Alan spoke.

"I am so blessed with my earthly family. That creek has become our symbol of a new life together. We are here to serve one another. Any treasures of this world are nothing compared to the riches and glory of heaven. My wife, Lucy, never gave up on me. Jake helped me to know that my Father in heaven never gave up on me either. I hope my story has encouraged you. Please greet us as we desire to get to know each one of you. Thank you."

Brandon hugged each member of the Wiley family and stepped up to the microphone.

"What an awesome testimony and message. Only a few months ago we started these gatherings, and I am blown away by the participation. God is, truly, at work in our midst. As Alan shared about the bench assembly process, I remember feeling that it would be impossible to

have them set up for this event. God handles the impossible with ease, don't you think?"

The audience stood and cheered loudly.

"I must confess that I did not know what the agenda for this evening would be, but I trusted God. I don't think I could have topped this. Thank you so much, Alan, for your inspired testimony."

"I must confess that I didn't think I could talk as long as I did, Brandon, but that was the message laid on my heart."

"I would ask the audience to continue to lift up the Wiley family in their prayers. If there are any other needs here, please let my father, Jake, or me, know, as we would love to add them to our prayer list. We feel that God has brought us together in this place to serve Him, and everyone attending tonight is part of our extended family."

Brandon closed with prayer and then had David lead in a few hymns. Brandon stood with the Wiley's as the people made their way to shake hands or offer thoughts. If anyone was going through hard times, it was not evident on his or her face. That night, for some, was an escape. For others, it was a time to enjoy family and friends. For the Wiley family, it was a new benchmark in their lives, which would bond them forever.

THE BREAKTHROUGH

Bob Edwards heard Alan's message, and it deeply pricked his heart. The death of his wife and his daughter's abandonment still plagued him. Alan's fatherly training left him feeling the pains of guilt, which could have consumed him, if not for the changing power of God in his life. Bob still harbored those feelings. Alan's message was a new source of hope. He stayed until most of the guests had left and approached Jake.

"Jake, got a moment?"

"You bet, Mr. Edwards, What's up?"

"Just call me Bob. That was a great message tonight. I think Alan should be a preacher. He had me riveted to my seat."

"That may have been the holy Spirit, Bob."

"No doubt. Anyway, do you remember my story?"

"I sure do, Bob. Brandon, Terry and I pray for you and your daughter daily. Has anything changed?"

"Not yet, Jake. But, somehow, I sense that it will soon. I still have not heard from Angel, but Alan's testimony spoke to my heart in a mighty way tonight. I think that God wants me to know that He is in control."

"I'm sure He is, Bob. You may not know where your daughter, Angel, is, but you can be certain that He does. If your heart was pricked tonight, then I have to think that you will get relief very soon."

"I hope so, Jake. I miss Angel so much. I lost her mother. I cannot imagine losing her as well. That would be more than I could take. I believe, like Alan, that our meeting was no accident. Those pallets, which you saw by the dumpster, have always been there, yet your eyes were open to see them that first day. By the way, I stopped getting nasty grams from the city about the clutter since you came along."

"God has a way of opening our eyes to see things that have always been there. It's like buying a new car. Suddenly, that model is everywhere on the road. Our new purchase opened our eyes to see them. When Brandon spoke about being called to have a family ministry involving a bonfire, my eyes were opened."

"That makes perfect sense. Now, I want my eyes to be opened to see again. I need a focus other than the pain and guilt that I have been harboring inside."

"Have you reached out to God and asked him, Bob?"

"I pray for relief every day."

"I mean, have you asked Him to be your personal Savior? Have you made Jesus Lord of your life?"

"I was brought up in a Christian home, went to church almost every Sunday, and was dedicated by my parents."

"Those are all good things, Bob, but you need to make a personal commitment. Jesus died a brutal death on a wooden cross for everyone. Do you know what sin is?"

"I believe that it is going against God."

"That's a good way of saying it. God hates sin. He desires to have fellowship with His creation without it. We have to come to a time in our lives when we recognize that we have turned away from God and deserve punishment. Romans 5:8 tell us that the wages of sin is death, *but the gift of God is eternal life. We deserve to die, but Christ died for us."*

"That's deep, Jake. Everyone dies."

"Everyone dies an earthly death. Jesus lets us know that there is life after death. We can spend eternity with God or without him. We need to make a choice."

"Of course, I would choose eternity with God."

"Then you must admit that you are a sinner, ask for forgiveness, and accept God's free gift of salvation through His son, Jesus Christ."

"I want to receive Him, Jake."

Jake knelt and led Bob in prayer. Bob concluded by accepting Jesus as his Savior. The men stood and embraced.

"Bob, I want you to consider being baptized. The creek in back is a great place."

"I feel as though a huge weight has been lifted off my shoulders. I can't explain it."

"We try so hard to accomplish things in this life on our own strength. Sometimes we get to the point that we just tire. All things are possible with God. You are now a new creation and have tapped into that power. If you were a power tool, then your run down battery pack has just been replaced with a fully charged one."

"It feels good. I would like to be baptized."

"Baptism tells the world that you are a child of God. I will ask the pastor to perform it."

"I would like you to baptize me."

"I guess that would be all right, although I have not baptized anyone before. Jesus commanded His disciples to perform that task. We should have witnesses, however. I will talk to my pastor about it. How would next Saturday be for you?"

"Let's plan on Saturday then."

After the two men prayed about the return of Angel into Bob's life, they parted ways. Jake called his pastor and discussed Bob's baptismal request. The time was set for six o'clock that Saturday at the creek. The congregation was alerted so many would come prior to the hayride and bonfire festivities.

Throughout the week, Jake could not stop thinking about Bob's daughter. Somehow, the thoughts of a baptism at the creek brought on additional thoughts about a miracle of reconciliation with Angel. God is a big God. Surely, heaven's storehouse of treasures would open as they did for Jake after his baptism, when his father re-entered his life. Could it be possible that a similar event would happen for Bob? Jake found himself praying continually for Angel and her father throughout the week. He shared his thoughts with Brandon, who also prayed for them.

Saturday seemed to arrive quickly. By five-thirty the people began to arrive at the farm to mark their places on the benches. The event had taken on great anticipation within the community. People heard about it from friends and were coming from well outside the city limits. Some came to see what all of the hoopla was about. Others came to be with friends or family living in the area. In any event, the people were arriving early, anticipating a large crowd.

Parking was posing a problem as well. The normal route for the hayride had to be shortened to allow for the additional cars. As the people arrived, Jake and Brandon tried to greet them. They reflected on just how far the bonfire approach to ministry had come.

"Can you believe the people, Dad?"

"Your ministry has come a long way, and quickly I might add."

"It's our ministry together."

"It's God's work, Son. It sure is amazing to watch Him work."

"That it is. I think He has something big planned again tonight. I can just feel it."

"We have seen lives changed here, especially our lives. I am so proud of you, Son. I abandoned you as a baby, much like my father

did with me when I was five years old. Now, I look at you and see a miracle."

"You may have abandoned me, but God never did. He stayed with both of us. He seems to enjoy using our own failures for a higher purpose."

"You are so right."

Bob arrived fifteen minutes before his scheduled baptism. The pastor arrived shortly afterwards and motioned for Brandon to join him at the creek. Brandon was prepared for his walk in the creek, wearing a pair of old shorts and a tee shirt he received from an event at the church with the teens. A microphone was hanging from the tree limb over the water. The crowd was instructed to make their way down to the creek to witness the ceremony.

Brandon received some instruction from his pastor, yet felt a bit uneasy about performing the baptism. The pastor assured him that everything was fine, and the butterflies stopped fluttering in his stomach. By the time the crowd gathered, Bob was in the water with Brandon.

"Bob and I would like to thank you all for coming tonight. This is a first for me, but I know that God approves. In a moment I will ask Bob a question, but I want each of you to ponder it in your own hearts as well. Bob, have you accepted Jesus Christ as your personal Savior and desire to be baptized in front of these witnesses?"

"I have and I do," Bob responded.

"Then I baptize you in the name of the Father, the Son, and the Holy Spirit."

Bob's head was gently placed under the water and then raised again. The audience erupted with an applause, which soothed Bob's ears.

"Today, you are a new creature in Christ, Bob. I am sure He has great things in store for you."

Immediately after Brandon spoke those words, he heard a voice from the back of the crowd. The clapping was loud, but somehow, the voice rose above the noise, despite the evidence of remorse. A young woman made her way through the crowd. From down in the creek, neither Bob nor Brandon could see her face. As she approached, however, Bob began to weep uncontrollably.

"What's wrong, Bob?" Brandon asked.
"Nothing is wrong. That's my Angel."
"Your daughter?'
"Yes, I know her voice anywhere."

Bob could not get out of the creek quickly enough. He heard the voice and ran toward it. The crowd opened up and he could see his daughter. The sun illuminated her hair with a glow that appeared heavenly.

"My Angel. My Angel."

Tears streamed down her father's face as Angela approached. The crowd quickly moved apart to allow the young lady to pass unobstructed. Her eyes were red from tears as well, but joy was on her face. No one doubted that God was working in a mighty way in their midst.

"Daddy, I am so sorry."

Bob opened his arms to receive her. His drenched clothing did not stop her from returning the embrace. The crowd sensed the joy and sighed. For several moments, Bob was speechless. Although many questions surfaced in his mind, the only thing that mattered was that his daughter had returned. His heart was overflowing with joy and praise.

"I missed you so much, Angel."
"I am so sorry that I abandoned you, Daddy."
"I am the one who should feel sorry. I let you down."
"I blamed you for mom's death. I could not bear to be near you."
"Your mother had some emotional problems. I think they were from her childhood, but she would not open up to me about what they

were. She would just lose it on occasion. I learned to wait until she calmed down. After she died, I blamed myself. I should have been more to help her. I thought that my love for her would be enough over time."

"Last week I met with some young people near the Cape where I have been living. They were members of the Youth for Christ group at a church there. Anyway, they began to share in a meeting. I felt convicted about something, but I did not understand why."

"The Holy Spirit spoke to me last week as well. That is why I was baptized today."

"That Spirit told me to seek forgiveness from you, but that is not what brought me here tonight. I didn't know that you would be here. The youth group heard about the bonfire and thought it would be fun to drive over and check it out."

"It's amazing how God works my child. He had all of this planned from the beginning."

"I am sure of that. I was sitting on the benches waiting for the activities at the creek to be completed, when I heard a voice call out your name. Immediately, I ran towards you."

Except for the brief introduction before the ceremony, Bob's name had not been mentioned. Bob knew that the voice she heard came directly from God. Their reunion would come after he was raised from the water. Whatever happened before was now washed clean. The people from her church were instruments to lead her to this place.

"I love you, Daddy. Please forgive me."
"Of course I forgive you, Angel. I love you."
"There's one more thing. I recommitted my life this week to Jesus. I would like to be baptized here tonight. Is that possible?"

Bob glanced over to Brandon who had made his way near them. He asked him if he would perform one more baptism, which Brandon agreed. The announcement was made and the ceremony was completed. Terry was about

Angel's size and brought down a change of clothes and some towels. The hayrides began.

Concluding Message

The evening left Jake and Brandon with many thoughts about how God was in total control. Brandon spent much of the time before leading the service thinking about all the events that led up to that time. God was working out every detail. Brandon could only see small portions of the bigger picture, while God had the whole canvas. The whole idea of having a bonfire on the farm for group ministry seemed odd at the time, but Brandon was faithful to follow through. Each potential obstacle was overcome.

The very first event led to prayers for two families. Now, both families were united and committed to a life of serving God. The benches served as a reminder of how one family came together. The cross, formed at the creek, provided a symbol for others. The sounds of happy children along with the smiles of parents added to the satisfaction that God must have been feeling. Serving the Lord was paying great dividends.

When the fire began to be only a light glow and the music started, everyone took his seat. The benches were full, and people found places on the grass to gather. The adults sang along with familiar hymns and choruses while many children offered sign language, which they learned in church. From Brandon's view on the stage; everyone was in a form of worship. When the music stopped, Brandon took the microphone and began to address the crowd.

"This has been an amazing evening."

The crowd agreed with a thunderous applause.

"When this ministry began, two families were placed on our prayer list, namely, the Wiley's and the Edwards'. Tonight we have witnessed God's answers in a truly phenomenal way."

Again the audience erupted for several minutes.

"As usual, I am addressing you without a preplanned script to follow. I have learned that God's script is far more effective than anything I can come up with. So, again, I will let His Spirit guide me. Before I begin, however, I want Bob and his daughter, Angel, to come up on stage for a moment."

Bob took Angel's hand and walked towards the stage. There was a youthful spring in his step; Angel did not appear embarrassed or uneasy. Although, neither of them knew what to expect, they walked up the stairs without hesitation. Brandon met them at the top of the stairs and embraced them. Then, they proceeded to the center where the mike was fixed to a stand.

"First, I want to say welcome to the family of God."

The crowd stood and cheered.

"We may not see the answers to our prayers in such a magnificent way, but we can be assured that God hears them. For those of you in prayer over loved ones, please know that God's timing is better than ours. Be patient."

Brandon paused.

"Second, I would like this audience to see how God worked in this family's life through this ministry. Tell us, Bob, how we met."

"I was about to leave my business when you and your dad showed up to inquire about the broken pallets stored near our trash dumpsters. My secretary called me about your inquiry."

"Was that unusual?"

"I'll say. Those pallets had been an eyesore for many months, perhaps even a year. Such an inquiry seemed strange."

"So how did you respond?"

"I was happy to get rid of them. You told me they would be used for a bonfire for family gatherings and I thought that was unusual in itself. I don't recall having events like that before, at least not here."

"So, the idea of a bonfire intrigued you?"

"I guess it did at that. My curiosity led me to attend your first burning, and I have been here every time since."

"You have also been a generous provider of marshmallows and other items. Thank you so much, Bob."

The crowd acknowledged his generosity with applause.

"Now, Angel, this is the first time you have been here. Is that correct?"

"Yes."

"So could you tell us what brought you here."

"An old Ford van." (She laughed) *"I met a Youth For Christ group of young people who befriended me. Their church heard of the event and decided to check it out."*

"How far away is that church?"

"About an hour's drive."

"So tell us Angel, did you think you would see your dad here?"

"Not in my wildest dreams. I knew he lived here, but that was not why I came. My friends thought it would be fun, and I joined them."

"How do you feel now?"

"Unbelievably happy. For the first time since my mother died, I feel whole again."

"Did anything else happen this past week?"

"Yes. On Monday I recommitted my life to Jesus. I had asked Him into my heart as a thirteen year old, but when mom died, I, well I gave up on God."

"He sure did not give up on you."

"He did not and I am so thankful."

"My friends, listen to me. When you feel that God has abandoned you, take heed. Examine your life and see if the one who left is you."

"I blamed my dad and God for mom's death. I may never know why she took her life, but I know that God was not the instrument. I pray that my mother is in His arms even now."

"So, here we have two different sets of circumstances that led this family back together. God can work through pallets of wood or people to accomplish great things. He can turn heartache into triumph if we allow Him to work. He is ever-present, omnipotent, and wants each of us to know Him in a personal way. Please, give a hand to this family and continue to pray that God will direct their paths."

The crowd stood in appreciation. Bob and his daughter waved as they proceeded back to their seats on the ground. God's Spirit was felt in their smiles.

"It seems as though we might have a problem in the future," Brandon continued. *"This farm is only so big, and the benches are completely full tonight."*

The audience voiced their approval once again with alleluias, stomping of feet on the bench flooring, and clapping. Then they sat down wondering what Brandon would say next. The last thing they wanted to hear was that the bonfires would stop.

"Dear friends, this is a good problem. We will continue to have bonfire events here, but we have received letters from other organizations, inquiring about how to get something like this started in their towns. Local fire departments and town boards are being

bombarded with requests for fire pits. I think we started something here."

Again, the crowd roared.

"We need to be in prayer for these places as well as our own. I plan on following God's leading in my life and, until something changes, this place will continue this ministry here. Yet, even if something happens that causes us to no longer meet, I think we have learned something wonderful. The human spirit thrives on interaction with others. We need to share our stories like the Wiley's and the Edwards'. Without that, we think that whatever we are going through is unique only to us. I would encourage you to gather together like the early church. Share together regularly. Pray together as often as God pricks your heart. Always be ready to follow God's call. Thank you for coming tonight, and may the God of all Creation bless you richly this week."

Jake could not wait to hug his son. His tears of joy streamed down his face. The son he abandoned had not only been restored in his life, but now had become the teacher. Jake could not imagine ever abandoning anyone again.

www.ingramcontent.com/pod-product-compliance
Lightning Source LLC
Chambersburg PA
CBHW021634120626
46545CB00002B/531